HUGH BLACK

HARVEST HOUSE PUBLISHERS
Eugene, Oregon 97402

Except where otherwise indicated, the Scripture quotations in this book are taken from the King James Version of the Bible.

Original edition Copyright 1898 by Fleming H. Revell Co.
Revised edition Copyright © 1986 by Harvest House Publishers
Eugene, Oregon 97402

Library of Congress Catalog Card Number 86-080711
ISBN 0-89081-513-5

Printed in the United States of America.

Friendship

Friendship is to be valued for what
there is in it, not for what can be gotten
out of it. When two people appreciate each
other because each has found the other
convenient to have around, they are
simply acquaintances with a business
understanding. To seek friendship for
its utility is as futile as to seek the end
of a rainbow for its bag of gold. A true
friend is always useful in the highest sense;
but we should beware of thinking of our
friends as brother members of a mutual-
benefit association, with its periodical
demands and threats of suspension for
non-payment of dues.

Trumbull

Contents

THE MIRACLE OF
FRIENDSHIP

CHAPTER ONE

The Miracle of Friendship

The idea so common in the ancient writers is not all a poetic conceit: that the soul of man is only a fragment of a larger whole, and goes out in search of other souls in which it will find its true completion. We walk among worlds unrealized until we have learned the secret of love. We know this, and in our sincerest moments admit this, even though we are seeking to fill up our lives with other ambitions and other hopes.

It is more than a dream of youth that there may be a satisfaction of the heart without which (and in comparison with which) all worldly success is failure. In spite of the

selfishness which seems to blight all of life,
our hearts tell us that there is possible a nobler
relationship of devotion.

Friendship in its accepted sense is not
the highest of the different grades in that
relationship, but it has its place in the kingdom of love, and through it we bring ourselves into training for a still larger love. The
natural man may be self-absorbed and self-
centered, but in a truer sense he will give up
self and link his life on to others. Hence the
joy with which he makes the great discovery
that he is something to another person and
another is everything to him.

The cynic may speak of the obsolete
sentiment of friendship, and he can find
much to justify his cynicism. Indeed, at first
blush, if we look at the relative place the
subject holds in ancient as compared with
modern literature, we might say that friendship is a sentiment that is rapidly becoming
obsolete. In pagan writers friendship takes a
much larger place than it now receives. The
subject looms large in the works of Plato,
Aristotle, Epictetus, and Cicero. In all the

ancient systems of philosophy, friendship was treated as an integral part of the system.

It is not easy to explain why its part in Christian ethics is so small in comparison. The change is due to an enlarging of the thought and life of man. Modern ideals are wider and more impersonal, just as the modern conception of the state is wider. The Christian ideal of love even for enemies has swallowed up the narrower ideal of philosophic friendship.

Yet friendship is not an obsolete sentiment. It is as true now as in Aristotle's time that no one would care to live without friends, though he had all other good things. It is still necessary to our life in its largest sense. The danger of sneering at friendship is that it may be discarded or neglected, not in the interests of a more spiritual affection, but to minister to a debased and cynical self-indulgence.

There is possible today, as ever, a generous friendship which forgets self. The history of the heart-life of man proves this. What records we have of this in the literature of every country! For a good man men have even dared to die. Mankind has been glorified by countless silent heroisms, by unselfish service and self-sacrificing love. Christ, who always took the highest ground in His estimate of men, and never once put man's capacity for the noble on a low level, made the high-water mark of human friendship the standard of His own great action: "Greater love hath no man than this, that a man lay down his life for his friends."

This high-water mark has often been reached. Men have given themselves to each other with nothing to gain, with no self-interest to serve, and with no keeping back part of the price. It is false history to base all of life on selfishness, to leave out of the list of human motives the highest motive of all. The miracle of friendship has been enacted on this dull earth of ours too often to allow us to doubt either its possibility or its wondrous beauty.

The classic instance of David and Jonathan represents the typical friendship. They met, and at the meeting knew each other to be nearer than kindred. By a certain sense of affinity they felt that they belonged to each other. Out of all the chaos of the time and the disorder of their lives there arose for these two men a new and beautiful world in which reigned peace and love and sweet content.

It was the miracle of the death of self. Jonathan forgot his pride, and David his ambition. It was as the smile of God changing the world to them. It saved one of them from the temptations of a squalid court and the other from the sourness of an exile's life. Jonathan's princely soul had no room for envy or jealousy. David's frank nature rose to meet the magnanimity of his friend.

In the kingdom of love there was no disparity between the king's son and the shepherd boy. The kind of gift that each gave and received is not to be bought or sold. It was the fruit of the innate nobility of both: It softened and tempered a very trying time for both. Jonathan withstood his father's anger to shield his friend, and David was patient with Saul for his son's sake. They agreed to be true to each other in their difficult position.

Close and tender must have been the bond, which had such fruit in princely gener-

The world thinks we idealize
our friend, and tells us that love
is proverbially blind. Not so—
it is only <u>love</u> that truly sees.

osity and mutual loyalty of soul. Fitting was the beautiful lament when David's heart was bereaved at tragic Gilboa: "I am distressed for thee, my brother Jonathan; very pleasant hast thou been unto me: thy love to me was wonderful, passing the love of women." Love is always wonderful, a new creation, fair and fresh to every loving soul. It is the miracle of spring to the cold and dull earth.

When Montaigne wrote his essay on friendship, he could do little but tell the story of his friend. The essay continually reverts to this, with joy that he had been privileged to have such a friend and with sorrow at his loss. It is a chapter of his heart. There was an element of necessity about it, as there is about all the great things of life. He could not account for it. It came to him without effort or choice. It was a miracle, but it happened. "If a man should importune me to give a reason why I loved him, I can only answer, because it was he, because it was I." It was as some secret appointment of heaven. They were both grown men when they first met, and death separated them soon after. "If I should compare all my life with the four years I had the happiness to enjoy the sweet society of this excellent man, it is nothing but smoke, an obscure and tedious night from the day that I lost him. I have led a sorrowful and languishing life ever since. I was so accustomed to be always his second in all places and in all interests that . . . I am now no more than half a man, and have but half a being."

The joy that comes from a true communion of heart with another person is perhaps one of the purest and greatest in the world, but its function is not exhausted by merely giving pleasure. Though we may not be conscious of it, there is a deeper purpose in it, an education in the highest arts of living. Even intellectually it means the opening of a door into the mystery of life. Only love truly understands, truly gives insight. We cannot truly know anything without sympathy, without getting out of self and entering into others. A man cannot be a true naturalist, and observe the ways of birds and insects accurately, unless he can watch long and lovingly. We can never *know* children unless we *love* them. Many of the chambers of the house of life are forever locked to us until love gives us the key.

To learn to love all kinds of nobleness gives insight into the true significance of things, and gives a standard to settle their relative importance. An uninterested spectator sees nothing, or, what is worse, sees wrongly. Most of our mean estimates of human nature in modern literature, and our false realisms in art, and our stupid pessimisms in philosophy, are due to an unintelligent reading of surface facts. Men set out to note and collate impressions without genuine interest in the lives they see, and therefore without true insight into them. They miss that inwardness which love alone can supply.

If we look without love we can only see the outside, the mere form and expression of the subject studied. Only with tender compassion and loving sympathy can we see the beauty even in the eye dull with weeping and in the fixed face pale with care. We will often see noble patience shining through them, and loyalty to duty, and virtues and graces unsuspected by other people.

The divine meaning of a true friendship is that it is often the first unveiling of the secret of love. It is not an end in itself, but has most of its worth in what it leads to: the priceless gift of seeing with the heart rather than with the eyes. To love one soul for its beauty and grace and truth is to open the way to appreciate all beautiful and true and gracious souls, and to recognize spiritual beauty wherever it is seen.

The possibility of friendship must be a faith with us. The cynical attitude is an offense. It is possible to find in the world truehearted and faithful dealing between man and man. To doubt this is to doubt the divine in life. In spite of all deceptions and disillusionments, in spite of all the sham fellowships, in spite of the flagrant cases of self-interest and callous cruelty, we must keep clear and bright our faith in the possibilities of our nature. The man who hardens his heart because he has been imposed upon has no real belief in virtue, and with suitable circumstances could become the deceiver instead of the deceived.

The great miracle of friendship with its infinite wonder and beauty may be denied to us, and yet we may believe in it. To believe that friendship is possible is enough, even though in its very best form it has never come to us. To possess it is to have one of the world's sweetest gifts.

Aristotle defines friendship as one soul abiding in two bodies. There is no explaining such a relationship, but there is no denying it either. It has not deserted the world since Aristotle's time. Some of our modern poets have sung of it with as brave a faith as any poet of old. What splendid monuments to friendship we possess in Milton's *Lycidas* and Tennyson's *In Memoriam!* In both there is the recognition of the spiritual power of it, as well as the joy and comfort it brought. The grief is tempered by an awed wonder and a glad memory.

The finest feature of Rudyard Kipling's work (and it is a constant feature of it) is the comradeship between commonplace soldiers of no high moral or spiritual attainment; it is the strongest force in their lives, and on occa-

The glory of life is to <u>love</u>,
not to be loved; to gi<u>ve</u>, not to
get; to <u>serve</u>, not to be served.
Love is the true miracle, and to
the one who loves come both
wonder and joy.

sion makes heroes of them. We feel that their faithfulness to each other is almost the only point at which their souls are reached. The threefold cord of his soldiers, vulgar in mind and common in thought as they are, is a cord which is not easily broken, and it is their friendship and loyalty to each other which save them from utter vulgarity.

In Walt Whitman there is the same insight into the force of friendship in ordinary life, with added wonder at the miracle of it. He is the poet of comrades, and sings the song of companionship more than any other theme. He ever comes back to the lifelong love of comrades. The mystery and the beauty of it impressed him.

> *O tan-faced prairie-boy,*
> *Before you came to camp*
> *came many a welcome gift,*
> *Praises and presents came*
> *and nourishing food,*
> *till at last among the recruits*
> *You came, taciturn,*
> *with nothing to give—*

THE MIRACLE OF FRIENDSHIP

We but looked on each other,
When lo! more than all the gifts
of the world you gave me.

After all, in spite of the vulgar materialism of our day, we do feel that the spiritual side of life is the most important, and brings the only true joy. And friendship in its essence is spiritual. It is the free, spontaneous outflow of the heart, and is a gift from the great Giver.

Friends are born, not made. At least it is so with the higher sort. The marriage of souls is a heavenly mystery, one which we cannot explain and need not try to explain. The method by which it is brought about differs very much, and depends largely on temperament. Some friendships grow, ripening slowly and steadily with the years. We cannot tell where they began, or how. They have become part of our lives, and we just accept them with sweet content and glad confidence. We have discovered that somehow we are rested and inspired by a certain companionship, that we understand and are understood easily.

Or it may come like love at first sight, by

the thrill of mutual affinity. This type is more uncertain, and needs to be tested and corrected by the trial of the years that follow. It has to be found out whether it is really spiritual kinship or mere emotional impulse. It is a matter of temper and character. A naturally reserved person finds it hard to open his heart, even when his instinct prompts him, while a sociable, responsive nature is easily companionable. It is not always this quick attachment, however, which wears best, and that is the reason why youthful friendships have the character of being so fickle. They are due to a natural, instinctive delight in society. Most young people find it easy to be agreeable, and are ready to place themselves under new influences.

But whatever the method by which a true friendship is formed, whether the growth of time or the birth of sudden sympathy, there seems to have been an element of necessity. It is a sort of predestined spiritual relationship. We speak of a man meeting his fate, and we speak truly. When we look back we see it to be like destiny: life converged to life, and there was no getting out of it even if we wished it. It is not that we made a choice, but that the choice made us. If it has come gradually, we waken to the presence of the force which has been in our life, and has come into it neither hastening nor resting, till now we know it to be an eternal possession. Or, as we are going about other business, never dreaming of the thing which occurs, the unexpected happens: On the road a light shines on us, and our life is never the same again.

In one of its aspects faith is the recognition of the inevitableness of providence; when it is understood and accepted, it brings a great consoling power into our life. We feel that we are in the hands of a love that orders our ways, and this knowledge means serenity and peace. The fatality of friendship is gratefully accepted, as is the fatality of birth. To the faith which sees love in all creation, all of life becomes harmony, and all sorts of loving relationships among men seem to be part of the natural order of the world. Indeed, such miracles are only to be looked for, and if absent from the life of man would make it hard to believe in the love of God.

The world thinks we idealize our friend, and tells us that love is proverbially blind. Not so—it is only *love* that truly sees. If we wonder what another man sees in his friend, it should be the wonder of humility, not the supercilious wonder of pride. He sees something which we are not permitted to witness. Beneath and among what looks only like worthless slag there may glitter the pure gold of a beautiful character. That anybody in the world should love us, and see in us not what colder eyes see (and not even what we are but what we may become), should make us humble and gentle in our criticism of other people's friendships. Our friends see the best in us, and by that very fact they call forth the best from us.

The great difficulty in this whole subject is that the relationship of friendship is so often one-sided. It seems strange that there should be so much unrequited affection in the world. It seems almost impossible to get a completely balanced union. One person gives so much more, and has to be content to get so much less. One of the most humiliating things in life is when another person seems to offer his friendship lavishly, but we are unable to respond. So much love seems to go begging. So few attachments seem complete. So much affection seems unrequited.

But are we sure it is unrequited? The difficulty is caused by our common selfish standards. Most people, if they had their choice, would prefer to be loved rather than to love, if only one of these alternatives were permitted. That springs from the root of selfishness in human nature, which makes us think that possession brings happiness. But the glory of life is to *love*, not to be loved; to *give*, not to get; to *serve*, not to be served. Love is the true miracle, and to the one who loves come both wonder and joy.

THE CULTURE OF FRIENDSHIP

CHAPTER TWO

The Culture of Friendship

The Book of Proverbs might almost be called a treatise on friendship, so full is it of advice about the kind of person a young man should consort with, and the kind of person he should avoid. It is full of shrewd, and prudent, and wise (sometimes almost worldly-wise) counsel. It is caustic in its satire about false friends, and about the way in which friendships are broken. "The rich hath many friends," with an easily understood implication concerning their quality. "Every man is a friend to him that giveth gifts," is its sarcastic comment on the ordinary motives of mean men. Its picture of the plausible, fickle, lip-praising, and time-serving man, who blesses his friend with a loud voice, rising early in the morning, is a delicate piece of satire.

The fragile connections among men, as easily broken as mended pottery, get illustrated in the mischief-maker who loves to divide men: "A whisperer separateth chief friends." There is keen irony here over the quality of ordinary friendship, as well as condemnation of the talebearer and his sordid soul.

This cynical attitude is so common that we hardly expect such a shrewd book to speak heartily of the possibilities of human friendship. Its object rather is to put youth on its guard against the dangers and pitfalls of social life. It gives sound commercial advice about avoiding becoming surety for a friend. It warns against the tricks and the cheats and the bad faith which swarmed in the streets of a city then, as they do still. It laughs, a little bitterly, at the thought that friendship can be as common as the eager, generous heart of youth imagines. It almost sneers at the gullibility of men in this whole matter: "He that maketh many friends doeth it to his own destruction."

And yet there is no book, even in classical literature, which so exalts the idea of friendship and is so anxious to have it truly valued and carefully kept. The worldly-wise warnings are after all in the interests of true friendship. To condemn hypocrisy is not, as is so often imagined, to condemn religion. To spurn the spurious is not to reject the true. A sneer at folly may be only a covert argument for wisdom. Satire is negative truth. The unfortunate thing is that most men who begin with wordly-wise philosophy also end there. They never get past the sneer.

Not so this wise book. In spite of its insight into the weakness of man, in spite of its frank denunciation of the common masquerade of friendship, it speaks of true friendship in words of beauty that have never been surpassed in all the many appraisements of this subject. "A friend loveth at all times, and a brother is born for adversity. Faithful are the wounds of a friend. Ointment and perfume rejoice the heart; so doth the sweetness of a man's friend by hearty counsel. Thine own friend and thy father's friend forsake not." These are not the words of a cynic, who has lost faith in man.

True, this golden friendship is not a common thing to be picked up in the street. It would not be worth much if it were. Like wisdom, it must be sought for as for hidden treasures, and to keep it demands care and thought. To think that every goose is a swan, that every new comrade is the man of your own heart, is to have a very shallow heart. Every casual acquaintance is not a hero. There are pearls of the heart, which cannot be thrown to swine.

Till we learn what a sacred thing a true friendship is, it is futile to speak of the culture of friendship. The man who wears his heart on his sleeve cannot wonder if crows peck at it! There ought to be a sanctuary to which few receive admittance. It is either great innocence or great folly (and in this connection the terms are almost synonymous) to open our arms to everybody to whom we are introduced.

The Book of Proverbs, as a manual on

friendship, gives as shrewd and caustic warnings as are needed, but it does not go to the other extreme and say that all men are liars, that no truth and faithfulness are to be found anywhere. There *is* a friend that sticketh closer than a brother, says this wisest of books. There is possible such a blessed relationship, a state of love and trust and generous comradehood, where a man feels safe to be himself because he knows that he will not easily be misunderstood.

The word "friendship" has been abased by applying it to low and unworthy uses, and so there is plenty of copy still to be gotten from life by the cynic and the satirist. The sacred name of friend has been bandied about till it runs the risk of losing its true meaning. Rossetti's words find their point in life:

> *Was it a friend or foe that spread these lies?*
> *Nay, who but infants question in such wise?*
> *'Twas one of my most intimate enemies.*

It is useless to speak of cultivating the great gift of friendship unless we make clear to ourselves what we mean by a friend. We make connections and acquaintances, and call them friends. We have few friendships because we are not willing to pay the price of friendship.

Like all other spiritual blessings, friendship comes to all of us at some time or other, but is often let slip. We have the opportunities, but we do not make use of them. Most people make friends easily enough, but few keep them. They do not give the subject the care and thought and trouble it requires and deserves. We want the pleasure of society without the duty. We would like to get the good of our friends without burdening ourselves with any responsibility about keeping them friends. The commonest mistake we make is that we spread our friendship over a mass, and have no depth of heart left. We lament that we have no staunch and faithful friend when in fact we have really not expended the love which produces such. We want to reap where we have not sown.

The secret of friendship is the secret of all spiritual blessing: The way to get is to give. The selfish in the end can never get anything but selfishness. The hard find hardness everywhere. As you mete, it is meted out to you.

Some people have a genius for friendship. That is because they are open, responsive, and unselfish. They truly make the most of life, for apart from their special joys, even intellect is sharpened by the development of the affections. No material success in life is comparable to success in friendship.

We really do ourselves harm by our selfish standards. There is an old Latin proverb which says that it is not possible for a man to love and at the same time to be wise. But this is only true when wisdom is made equal to prudence and selfishness, and when love is made the same. Rather, it is never given to a man to be wise in the truest and noblest sense until he is carried out of himself in the purifying passion of love or the generosity of friendship. The self-centered person cannot keep friends even when he makes them; his selfish sensitiveness is always in the way, like a diseased nerve ready to be irritated.

The culture of friendship is a duty, as every gift represents a responsibility. It is also

Attention to detail is the secret
of success in every sphere of life.
Little kindnesses, little acts
of consideration, little
appreciations, and little
confidences are all that most
of us are called on to perform,
but they are all that are needed
to keep a friendship sweet.

a necessity, for without watchful care it can no more remain with us than can any other gift. Without culture it is at best only a potentiality. We may let it slip, or we can use it to bless our lives. The miracle of friendship, which came at first with its infinite wonder and beauty, wears off, and the glory fades into the light of common day. The early charm passes, and the soul forgets the first exaltation.

We are always in danger of mistaking the common for the commonplace. We must not look upon friendship merely as a great luxury of life, or it will cease to be even that. It begins with emotion, but if it is to remain it must become a habit. Habit is fixed when an accustomed thing is organized into life. Whatever the origin of friendship, it must become a habit or else it is in danger of passing away as other impressions have done before.

Friendship needs delicate handling. We can ruin it by stupid blundering at its very birth, and we can kill it by neglect. It is not every flower that has vitality enough to grow in stony ground. Lack of reticence, which is the outward sign of lack of reverence, is responsible for the death of many a good friendship. Worse still, it is often blighted at the very beginning by the insatiable desire for provocative conversation, which can forget the sacredness of confidence. Nothing is given to the man who is not worthy to possess it, and the shallow heart can never know the joy of a friendship, for he is not able to fulfill its essential conditions. It is also true that from the man that hath not is taken away even that which he hath.

The right method for the culture of friendship finds its best and briefest summary in the Golden Rule. To do to and for your friend what you would have him do to and for you is a simple summary of the whole duty of friendship. The very first principle of friendship is that it is a mutual thing, among spiritual equals, and therefore claims reciprocity, mutual confidence, and faithfulness. There must be sympathy to keep in touch with each other, but sympathy needs to be constantly exercised. It is a channel of communication which has to be kept open or else it will soon be clogged and closed.

The practice of sympathy may mean the cultivation of similar tastes, though this will almost naturally follow from the fellowship. But to cultivate similar tastes does not imply absorption of one of the partners or of the identity of both. Rather, part of the charm of friendship lies in the difference which exists in the midst of agreement. What is essential is that there be a real desire and a genuine effort to understand each other. It is well worthwhile to take pains to preserve a relationship so full of blessing to both parties.

Here, as in all relationships, is ample opportunity for patience. When we think of our own need for the constant exercise of this virtue, we will admit its necessity for other people. After the first flush of communion has passed, we must see in a friend things which detract from his worth, and perhaps things which irritate us. This is only to say that no one is perfect. With tact, and tenderness, and patience we may have the opportunity to help remove certain flaws in a fine character.

In any case it is foolish to forget the great virtues of our friend in fretful irritation at a few blemishes. We can keep the first ideal in our memory even if we know that it is not yet an actual fact. We must not let our friendship be coarsened, but must keep it sweet and delicate, that it may remain a refuge from the coarse world, a sanctuary where we leave criticism outside and breathe freely.

Trust is the first requisite for making a friend. How can we be anything but alone if our attitude toward people is one of armed neutrality—if we are suspicious, assertive, fretful, and overcautious in our advances? Suspicion kills friendship. There must be some magnanimity and openness of mind before a friendship can be formed. We must be willing to give ourselves freely and unreservedly.

Some people find it easier than others to make advances because they are naturally more trustful. A beginning has to be made somehow, and if we are moved to enter into friendship with another person, we must not be too cautious in displaying our feeling. If we stand off in cold reserve, the ice, which trembled toward thawing, is gripped again by the black hand of frost.

There may be a golden moment which has been lost through a foolish reserve. We are so afraid of giving ourselves away cheaply (and it is a proper enough feeling, the value of which we learn through sad experience), but on the whole the warm nature, which acts on impulse, is a better type than the overcautious nature, ever on the watch lest it commit itself. We can do nothing with each other—we cannot even do business with each other—without a certain amount of trust. Much more necessary is it in the beginning of a deeper friendship.

If trust is the first requisite for making a friend, *faithfulness* is the first requisite for keeping him. The way to have a friend is to be a friend. Faithfulness is the fruit of trust. We must be ready to lay hold of every opportunity which occurs for serving our friend. For most of us, life is made up of little things, and many a friendship withers through sheer neglect. Hearts are alienated because each is waiting for some great occasion for displaying

Friendship cannot be
permanent unless it becomes
spiritual. There must be
fellowship in the deepest things
of the soul, community in the
highest thoughts, sympathy with
the best endeavors.

affection. The great spiritual value of friendship lies in the opportunities it affords for service, and if these are neglected it is only to be expected that the gift should be taken from us. Friendship, though it begins with sentiment, will not live and thrive on sentiment. There must also be loyalty, which finds expression in service. It is not the greatness of the help or the intrinsic value of the gift which gives it worth, but rather its love and thoughtfulness.

Attention to detail is the secret of success in every sphere of life. Little kindnesses, little acts of consideration, little appreciations, and little confidences are all that most of us are called on to perform, but they are all that are needed to keep a friendship sweet. Such thoughtfulness keeps our sentiment in evidence to both parties. If we never show our kind feeling, what guarantee has our friend, or even ourself, that it exists?

Faithfulness in deed is the outward result of constancy of soul, which is the rarest and greatest of virtues. If there has come to us the miracle of friendship, if there is a soul to which our soul has been drawn, it is surely worthwhile being loyal and true. Through the little occasions for helpfulness we are training for the great trial, if it should ever come, when the fabric of friendship will be tested to its very foundation. The culture of friendship, and its abiding worth, never found nobler expression than in the beautiful proverb, "A friend loveth at all times, and a brother is born for adversity."

Most men do not deserve such a gift from heaven. They look upon it as a convenience, and accept the privilege of love without the responsibility of it. They even use their friends for their own selfish purposes, and so never have true friends. Some men shed friends at every step they rise in the social scale. It is mean and contemptible to merely use people only so long as they further one's personal interests.

But there is a nemesis on such heartlessness: To such people can never come the ecstasy and comfort of mutual trust. This worldly policy can never truly succeed. It stands to reason that they cannot have brothers born for adversity, and cannot count on the joy of the love that loves at all times, for they do not possess the quality which secures it. To act on the worldly policy, to treat a friend as if he might become an enemy, is of course to be friendless. To sacrifice a tried and trusted friend for any personal advantage of gain or position is to deprive our own heart of the capacity for friendship.

The passion for novelty will sometimes lead a man to act like this. Some shallow minds are ever afflicted by a craving for new experiences. They are the easy victims of the untried, and yearn perpetually for novel sensations. In this matter of friendship they are always ready to forsake the old for the new. They are always finding a swan in every goose they meet. They have their reward in a widowed heart. Says Shakespeare in his great manner:

> *The friends thou hast and their adoption tried*
> *Grapple them to thy soul with hoops of steel,*
> *But do not dull thy palm with entertainment*
> *Of each new-hatched, unfledged comrade.*

The *culture* of friendship must pass into

the *consecration* of friendship if it is to reach its goal. It is a natural development. Friendship cannot be permanent unless it becomes spiritual. There must be fellowship in the deepest things of the soul, community in the highest thoughts, sympathy with the best endeavors. We are bartering foolishly if we look on friendship merely as a luxury, and not as a spiritual opportunity. It is, or can be, an occasion for growing in grace, for learning love, for training the heart to patience and faith, for knowing the joy of humble service. We are throwing away our chance if we are not striving to be an inspiring and healthful environment to our friend. We are called to be our best to our friend, that he may be his best to us, bringing out what is highest and deepest in the nature of both of us.

The culture of friendship is one of the approved instruments of culture of the heart, without which a man has not truly come into his kingdom. It is often only the beginning, but through tender and careful culture it may be an education for the larger life of love. It broadens out in ever-widening circles, from the particular to the general, and from the general to the universal—from the individual to the social, and from the social to God.

The test of religion is ultimately a very simple one: If we do not love those whom we have seen, we cannot love those whom we have not seen. All our sentiment about people at a distance, and our heart-stirrings for the distressed and oppressed, and our prayers for the heathen, are pointless and fraudulent if we are neglecting those occasions for serving which lie close at hand. If we do not love our brethren here, how can we love our brethren elsewhere, except as a pious sentimentality? And if we do not love those we have seen, how can we love God whom we have not seen?

This is the highest function of friendship, and the reason why it needs thoughtful culture. We should be led to God by the joy of our lives as well as by the sorrow, by the light as well as by the darkness, by human fellowship as well as by human loneliness. He is the Giver of every good gift. We wound His heart of love when we sin against love.

The more we know of Christ's spirit, and the more we think of the meaning of God's fathomless grace, the more we will be convinced that the way to please the Father and to follow the Son is to cultivate the graces of kindness and gentleness and tenderness, to give ourselves to the culture of the heart. Not in the ecclesiastical arena, not in polemic for a creed, not in self-assertion and disputings do we please our Master best, but in the simple service of love. To seek the good of men is to seek the glory of God. These are not two things, but one and the same.

To be a strong hand in the dark to another in the time of need, to be a cup of strength to a human soul in a crisis of weakness, is to know the glory of life. To be a true friend, saving his faith in man and making him believe in the existence of love, is to save his faith in God. And such service is possible for all. We need not wait for the great occasion and for the exceptional opportunity. We can never be without our chance if we are ready to keep the miracle of love green in our hearts by humble service.

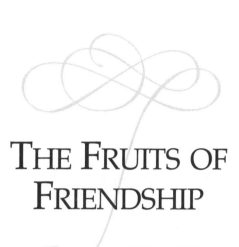

THE FRUITS OF FRIENDSHIP

CHAPTER THREE

The Fruits
of Friendship

I n our utilitarian age things are judged
by their practical value. People ask
of everything, What is its use? Nothing is held to be outside criticism, neither the
law because of its authority nor religion because of its sacredness. Every relationship in
life has been questioned, and is asked to show
the reason of its existence. Even relationships
like marriage, long held to be above question,
are put into the crucible.

Criticism is inevitable, and ought to be
welcomed, provided that we are careful about
the true standard to apply. When we judge a
thing by its use, we must not have a narrow
view of what utility is. Usefulness to man is

not confined to mere material values. The common standards of the marketplace cannot be applied to the whole of life. The things which cannot be bought cannot be sold, and the keenest evaluator would be puzzled to put a price on some of these unmarketable wares.

When we seek to show what are the fruits of friendship, we may be said to put ourselves in line with the critical spirit of our age. But even if it were proven that a man could make more of his life materially by himself if he gave no hostages to fortune, it would not follow that it is well to disentangle oneself from the common human bonds, for our caveat would here apply: that utility is larger than mere material gain.

But even from this point of view friendship justifies itself. Two are better than one, for they have a good reward for their labor. The principle of association in business is now accepted universally. Most of the world's business is done by companies, or partnerships, or associated endeavor of some kind. And the closer the intimacy between the people so engaged, the better the chance for success. Two are better than one even from the point of view of the reward of each. A threefold cord is not quickly broken, whereas a single strand may snap.

When people first learned, even in its most rudimentary sense, that union is strength, the blossoming of civilization began. For offense and for defense, the principle of association early proved itself the best strategy for survival. The future is always with Isaac, not with Ishmael; with Jacob, not with Esau. In everything this is seen: in the struggle of races, in trade, in ideas.

It is not necessary to labor the point that two are better than one, for a commercial age like ours at least knows its arithmetic. By the law of addition it is double, and by the law of multiplication twice the number. But it is neither so exact as that nor so self-evident. When we are dealing with people, our rules do not always work out correctly. In this area one and one are not always two. They are sometimes more than two and sometimes less than two.

Union of all kinds may be strength and may also be weakness. It was not till Gideon weeded out his army once and even twice that he was promised victory. The fruits of friendship may be corrupting and unspeakably evil to the life. The reward of the labor of two may be less than that of one. The boy pulling a wheelbarrow is lucky if he gets another boy to shove behind, but if the boy behind not only ceases to shove but sits on the barrow, the end result is worse than before. A threefold cord with two of the strands rotten is worse than a single sound strand, for it deceives us into putting too much weight on it.

In social economics it is evident that society is not merely the sum of the units that compose it. Two are better than one not merely because the force is doubled. It may even be said that two are better than two. Two together mean more than two added singly, for a new element is introduced which increases the power of each person individually.

When the man Friday came into the life of Robinson Crusoe, he brought with him a great deal more than his own individual value, which with his lower civilization would not be very much. But to Robinson Crusoe he represented society, and all the possibilities of social polity. It meant also the satisfaction of the social instincts, the play of the affections, and made Crusoe a different man. The two living together were more than the two living apart on different desert islands.

The truth of this strange contradiction of the multiplication table is seen in the relationship of friends. Each gives to the other and each receives, and the fruit of the friendship is more than either in himself possesses. Every individual relationship has contact with a universal. To reach out to the fuller life of love is a divine blessing because it leads to more than itself, and is the open door into the mystery of life. We feel ourselves united to the race, no longer isolated units but part of the sweep of the great social forces which mold mankind. Every bond which binds man to man is a new argument for the permanence of life itself, and gives a new insight into its meaning. Love is the pledge and the promise of the future.

Besides this sweeping benefit there are many practical fruits of friendship to the individual. These may be classified and subdivided almost endlessly, and indeed in every special friendship the fruits of it will differ according to the character and closeness of the tie, and according to the particular gifts of each of the partners. One man can give to his friend some quality of sympathy, or some kind of help, or can supply some social need which is lacking in his character or circumstances. Perhaps it is not possible to get a better division of the subject than the three noble fruits of friendship which Bacon enumerates: peace in the affections, support of the judgment, and aid in all actions and occasions.

First there is the *satisfaction of the heart*. We cannot live a self-centered life without feeling that we are missing the true glory of life. We were made for social interchange, if only that the highest qualities of our nature might have an opportunity for development. The joy which a true friendship gives reveals the existence of the lack of it, perhaps previously unfelt. It is a sin against ourselves to let our affections wither. This sense of incompleteness is an argument in favor of its possible satisfaction; our need is an argument for its fulfillment.

Our hearts demand love as truly as our bodies demand food. We cannot live suspiciously among people, careful of our own interests and fighting for our own hand, without doing dishonor and hurt to our own nature. To be for ourselves puts the whole world against us. To harden our heart hardens the heart of the universe.

We need sympathy, and therefore we crave for friendship. Even the most perfect of the sons of men felt this need of fellowship of the heart. Christ, in one sense the most self-contained of men, showed this human longing all through His life. He ever desired opportunities for enlargement of heart—in His disciples, in an inner circle within the circle, in the household of Bethany. "Will ye also go away?" He asked in the crisis of His career. "Could ye not watch with me one hour?" He sighed in His great agony. Though divine, He was also perfectly human, and therefore felt the lack of friendship.

No fellowship is true and real which does not elevate and promote nobility of conduct and strength of character. It should give a new zest to duty and a new inspiration to all that is good.

The higher our relationships with each other, the closer the fellowship demanded. Highest of all in the things of the soul, we feel that the true Christian life cannot be lived in the desert, but must be a life among fellowmen, and this because it is a life of joy as well as of service. We feel that, for the rounding of our life and the completion of our powers, we need fellowship with our kind. Stunted affections dwarf the whole person. We live by admiration, hope, and love, and these can be developed only in the social life.

The sweetest and most stable pleasures in life are never selfish. They are derived from fellowship, from common tastes and mutual sympathy. Sympathy is not a quality needed merely in adversity; it is needed as much when the sun shines. Indeed, it is more easily obtained in adversity than in prosperity. It is comparatively easy to sympathize with a friend's failure even though we are not so truehearted about his success. When a man is down in his luck, he can be sure of at least a certain amount of good fellowship to which he can appeal.

It is difficult to keep a little touch of malice or envy out of congratulations. It is sometimes easier to weep with those who weep than to rejoice with those who rejoice. This difficulty is felt not with people who are above us or have with little connection with us, but with our equals. When a friend succeeds, there may be a certain regret which is due to a fear that he is getting beyond our reach, passing out of our sphere, and perhaps will not need or desire our friendship so much as before.

It is a dangerous feeling to give way to, but up to a certain point it is natural and legitimate. A perfect friendship would not have room for such grudging sympathy, but would rejoice more for the other's success than for his own. The envious, jealous man never can be a friend. His mean spirit of detraction and insinuating ill-will kills friendship at its birth. Plutarch records a witty remark about Plistarchus, who was told that a notorious railer had spoken well of him. "I'll lay my life," said he, "somebody has told him I am dead, for he can speak well of no man living."

For true satisfaction of the heart there

must be a fount of sympathy for all the vicissitudes of life. Sorrow asks for sympathy, aches to let its griefs be known and shared by a kindred spirit. To find such is to dispel the loneliness from life. To have a heart which we can trust, and into which we can pour our griefs and our doubts and our fears, is already to take the edge from grief, the sting from doubt, the shade from fear.

Joy also demands that its joy should be shared. The man who has found his sheep that was lost calls together his neighbors and bids them rejoice with him because he has found the sheep that was lost. Joy is more social than grief. Some forms of grief desire only to creep away into solitude like a wounded beast to its lair, to suffer and die alone. But joy finds its counterpart in the sunshine and the flowers and the birds and the little children, and enters easily into all the movements of life. Sympathy will respond to a friend's gladness as well as vibrate to his grief. A simple, generous friendship will add to the joy and divide the sorrow.

The Christian life is preeminently a life of

friendship. It is individual in its root and social in its fruits. It is when two or three are gathered together that Christianity becomes a fact for the world. The joy of Christ will not be hid and buried in a man's own heart. "Come, see a man that told me all that ever I did" is the natural outcome of the first wonder and the first faith. It spreads from soul to soul by the impact of soul on soul, from the original impact of the great soul of God.

Christ's ideal is that of men banded together in a common cause, under common laws, serving the same purpose of love. It is meant to take effect upon man in all his social relationships—in the home, in the city, and in the state. Its greatest triumphs have been made through friendship, and it in turn has ennobled and sanctified the bond.

The growth of Christ's kingdom depends on the sanctified working of the natural ties among men. It was so at the very start: John the Baptist pointed out Christ to John the future Apostle and to Andrew; Andrew found his own brother Simon Peter; Philip found Nathaniel; and so society through its network of relations took into its heart the new message. The man who has been healed must go and tell those who are at home, must declare it to his friends and seek that they also should share in his great discovery.

The very existence of the church as a body of believers is due to this necessity of our nature, which demands opportunity for the interchange of Christian sentiment. The deeper the feeling, the greater is the joy of sharing it with another person. There is a wondrous enjoyment which comes from true intimacy of heart and close communion of soul, and the result is more than mere fleeting joy. When it is shared in the deepest thoughts and highest aspirations, when it is built on a common faith and lives by a common hope, it brings perfect peace. No friendship has done its work until it reaches the supremest satisfaction of spiritual communion.

Besides this satisfaction of the heart, friendship also gives *satisfaction of the mind*. Most people have a certain natural hesitance in coming to conclusions and forming opinions for themselves. We rarely feel confident until we have secured the agreement of other people in whom we trust. There is always a personal equation in all our judgments, so that we feel that they must be amended by comparison with those of other people.

We all realize the advantage of taking counsel. To ask for advice is a benefit whether we follow the advice or not. Indeed, the best benefit often comes from the opportunity of testing our own opinion and finding it valid. Sometimes the very statement of the case is enough to prove it one thing or the other. An advantage is reaped from a sympathetic listener even if our friend is unable to clarify the matter by his own special experience. Friends in counsel gain much intellectually. They acquire something approaching a standard of judgment, and are able to classify opinions and make up their mind more accurately and securely. By talking a subject over with another person we get fresh sidelights into it; new avenues open up and the whole question becomes larger and richer. Bacon says, "Friendship maketh daylight in the understanding, out of darkness and confusion of thoughts."

We may have been struck with the brilliance of our own conversation and the profundity of our own thoughts when we shared them with someone with whom we were in sympathy at the time. But the brilliance was not ours; it was the reflex action which was the result of the communion. That is why the effect of different people upon us is different, one making us creep into our shell and making us almost unable to utter a word, and another through some strange magnetism enlarging the bounds of our whole being and drawing the best out of us. The true insight after all is love. It clarifies the intellect and opens the eyes to much that was obscure.

Besides the subjective influence, there may be the great gain of honest counsel. A faithful friend can be trusted not to speak merely soft words of flattery. It is often the spectator who sees most of the game, and, if the spectator is at the same time keenly interested in us, he can have a more unbiased opinion than we can possibly have. He may have to wound our self-esteem, and he may

When men face the world
together, and are ready to stand
shoulder to shoulder, the sense
of comradeship makes each
strong. This help may not often
be called into play, but just to
know that it is there if needed
is a great comfort—to know
that if one falls the other
will lift him up.

have to speak for correction rather than for commendation, but "faithful are the wounds of a friend." The flatterer will take good care not to offend our susceptibilities by too many shocks of wholesome truth-telling; but a friend will seek our good, even if he must say the thing we hate to hear at the time.

This does not mean that a friend should always be plain spoken. Some people take advantage of what they call a true interest in our welfare in order to rub gall into our wounds. The man who boasts of his frankness and of his hatred of flattery is usually not frank—only brutal. A true friend will never needlessly hurt, but also will never let occasions slip by through cowardice. To speak the truth in love takes off the edge of unpleasantness which so often is found in truth-speaking. However much the wound may smart, in the end we are thankful for the faithfulness which caused it. "Let the righteous smite me; it shall be a kindness. Let him reprove me; it shall be an excellent oil, which shall not break my head."

In our relations with each other there is usually more advantage to be reaped from friendly encouragement than from friendly correction. True criticism does not consist in *depreciation* but in *appreciation*, in putting oneself sympathetically in another person's position and seeking to value the real worth of his work. There are more lives spoiled by undue harshness than by undue gentleness. More good work is lost from lack of appreciation than from too much of it, and certainly it is not the function of friendship to do the critic's work. Unless carefully repressed, such a spirit becomes censorious or spiteful, and has often been the means of losing a friend. It is possible to be kind without giving crooked counsel or oily flattery, and it is possible to be true without magnifying faults and indulging in cruel rebukes.

Besides the joy of friendship and its aid in matters of counsel, another of its noble fruits is the direct help it can give us in the difficulties of life. It gives strength to our character. It sobers and steadies us through our responsibility for each other which it entails. When men face the world together, and are ready to stand shoulder to shoulder, the sense

of comradeship makes each strong. This help
may not often be called into play, but just to
know that it is there if needed is a great comfort—to know that if one falls the other will
lift him up.

Sentiment does not amount to much if it
is not an inspiring force to lead to gentle and
generous deeds when there is need. The fight
is not so hard when we know that we are not
alone, but that there are some who think of us
and pray for us, and would gladly help us if
they got the opportunity.

Comradeship is one of the finest facts
and one of the strongest forces in life. A mere
strong man, however capable and however
successful, is of little account by himself.
There is no glamour of romance in his career.
The kingdom of romance belongs to David,
not to Samson—to David, with his eager, im-
petuous, affectionate nature, for whom three
men went in the jeopardy of life to bring him
a drink of water, and all for love of him.

Robertson of Brighton exclaims, "How
rare it is to have a friend who will defend you
thoroughly and boldly!" Yet that is just one of

the loyal things a friend can do. Some things which need to be said or done cannot be undertaken without indelicacy by the person concerned, and the keen instinct of a friend should tell him that he is needed. A little thoughtfulness would often suggest things that could be done for our friends, things that would make them feel that the tie which binds us to them is a real one. That man is rich indeed who possesses thoughtful, tactful friends with whom he feels safe when present and in whose hands his honor is secure when absent.

If there is no loyalty, there can be no great friendship. Most of our friendships lack the distinction of greatness because we are not ready for little acts of service. Without these our love dwindles down to a mere sentiment, and ceases to be the inspiring force for good to both lives which it was at the beginning.

The aid we may receive from friendship may be of an even more subtly powerful nature than material help: It may be a safeguard against temptation. The recollection of a friend whom we admire is a great force to save us from evil and to prompt us to good. The thought of his sorrow in any moral breakdown of ours will often embolden us to stand firm: What would my friend think of me if I did this or consented to this meanness? Could I look him in the face again and meet the calm pure gaze of his eye? Would my act be a blot on our friendship, and draw a veil over our fellowship? No friendship is true and real which does not elevate and promote nobility of conduct and strength of character. It should give a new zest to duty and a new inspiration to all that is good.

Influence is the greatest of all human gifts, and we all have it in some measure. There are some people to whom we are something, if not everything. There are some who are grappled to us with hoops of steel. There are some over whom we have ascendancy, or at least to whom we have access, who have opened the gates of the City of Mansoul to us, some we can sway with a word, a touch, a look. It must always be a solemn thing for a person to ask what he has done with this awesome power of influence. For what has our friend to be indebted to us—for good or for evil? Have we put on his armor and sent him out with courage and strength to the battle? Or have we dragged him down from the heights to which he once aspired? We are face to face here with the tragic possibilities of human relationships. In all friendship we open the gates of the city, and those who have entered must be either allies in the fight or treacherous foes.

All the fruits of friendship, whether blessed or hurtful, spring from this root of influence, and influence in the long run is the impress of our real character on other lives. Influence cannot rise above the level of our lives. The result of our friendship on other persons will ultimately be conditioned by the sort of persons we ourselves are. It adds a very sacred responsibility to life. Here indeed a good tree brings forth good fruit, but a corrupt tree brings forth evil fruit.

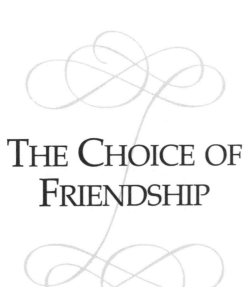

THE CHOICE OF
FRIENDSHIP

CHAPTER FOUR

The Choice
of Friendship

O ur responsibility for our friendships is not confined to making sure that our influence over other people is for good; we also have a duty to ourselves. As we possess the gift of influence over others, so we in turn are affected by every life which touches ours. Influence is like an atmosphere exhaled by each separate personality. Some people seem neutral and colorless, with no atmosphere to speak of. Some have a bad atmosphere, like the poisonous odor of noxious weeds. If our moral sense were keen and true we would instinctively know them, as some children do, and dread their company.

Other people have a good atmosphere; we can breathe there in safety and have a joyful sense of security. With some of these it is a delicate environment—sweet and suggestive, like the aroma of wild violets: We have to look, and sometimes even stoop, to get into its range. With some people it is like a pine forest, or a eucalyptus grove of warmer climates, which perfumes a whole countryside. It is good to know such: Christ's little ones and Christ's great ones. They put oxygen into the moral atmosphere, and we breathe more freely for it. They give us new insight, and fresh courage, and purer faith; by the impulse of their example they inspire us to nobler living.

There is nothing so important as the choice of friendship, for it both reflects character and affects it. A man is known by the company he keeps. This is an infallible test, for his thoughts, desires, ambitions, and loves are revealed here. He gravitates naturally to his congenial sphere. And it affects character, for it is the atmosphere he breathes. It enters his blood and makes the circuit of his veins. "All love assimilates to what it loves."

A man is molded into the likeness of the lives that come nearest him. It is at the point of the emotions that he is most impressionable. The material surroundings affect him, but the higher functions of life may be served in almost any external circumstances. Yet the environment of other lives and the communion of other souls are far more potent facts. The nearer people are to each other, and the less disguise there is in their relationship, the more invariably will the law of spiritual environment act.

It seems a tragedy that people who see each other as they are become like each other. But the principle carries as much hope in it as despair. If through it evil works havoc, through it also good persists. If we are hindered by the weakness of our associates, we are often helped by their goodness and sweetness. Contact with a strong nature inspires us with strength. Someone once asked Kingsley what was the secret of his strong and joyous life, and he answered, "I had a friend." If every evil man is a center of contagion, every good man is a center of healing. He provides an environment in which other people can see God.

Goodness creates an atmosphere for other souls to be good. It is a priestly garment that has virtue even for the finger that touches it. The earth has its salt and the world has its light in the sweet souls and winsome lives and Christlike characters to be found in it. The choice of friends is therefore one of the most serious affairs in life, because a man becomes molded into the likeness of what he loves in his friend.

From the purely selfish standard, every fresh tie we form means giving a new hostage to fortune and adding a new risk to our happiness. Apart from any moral evil, every intimacy is a danger of another blow to the heart. But if we desire fullness of life, we cannot help ourselves. A man may make many a friendship to his own hurt, but the isolated life is a greater danger still. Every relationship means risk, but we must take the risk, for while nearly all our sorrows come from our connection with other people, nearly all our joys have the same source. We need the knowledge and care and forethought to enable us to make the best of the necessities of our nature, and foremost of these is our choice of friends.

We may err on the one side by being too cautious and too exclusive in our attachments. We may be supercilious and disdainful in our estimate of men. Contempt always blinds the eyes. Every man is vulnerable somewhere, if only like Achilles in the heel. The true secret of insight is not *contempt* but *sympathy*. Such disdain usually means putting all the eggs into one basket, so that a smash spells ruin.

The other extreme is the attitude which easily makes many friends without much consideration of quality. We all know the type of man who is friendly with everybody but a true friend of none. He takes up with every sort of casual comrade and seeks to be on good terms with everybody. He makes what is called "good company" and is a favorite on all light occasions. His affections spread themselves out over a large expanse. He is easily consoled for a loss and easily attracted by a new attachment. And as he deals, so is he dealt with. Many people like him but few fully trust him. He makes many friends but is not particular about their quality.

The law of spiritual environment plays upon such a man with is relentless force. He gives himself away too cheaply, and opens himself to all sorts of influence. He is constantly laying himself in the way of temptation, and the evil example of some of his intimates gradually breaks down the barriers of his past training and teaching. The desire to please a crowd means that principle is let slip and conscience ceases to be his standard of action. His very friends are not true friends at all, being mostly of the fair-weather variety.

Though it may seem difficult to avoid either of these two extremes, we must not refuse to choose at all, and thereby leave things to chance. We sometimes drift into our connections with people, but the art of seamanship is tested by sailing and not by drifting. The subject of the choice of friendship is not advanced much by just letting people choose us as friends. That is to become the victim and not the master of our circumstances. While it is true that we are acted on as much as we act, and are chosen as much as we choose, it is not permitted to anyone merely to be passive, except at great cost.

We cannot go about with a touchstone testing all the people we meet until we find the ore that responds to our particular magnet. From one point of view we are absolutely passive: Things arrange themselves without effort, and by some subtle affinity we learn that we have gained a friend. The history of every true friendship is the brief description of Emerson: "My friends have come to me unsought; the great God gave them to me." There is an element of necessity in this, as in all crises of life.

Does it seem absurd and useless to speak about the choice of friendship? It should not, because the principles we set before ourselves will determine the kind of friends we have, as truly as if the whole initiative lay with us. We are chosen for the same reason for which we would choose. To try to separate the two processes is to make the same futile distinction, on a lower scale, between choosing God and being chosen by Him.

The value of having some definite principle by which to test friendship is not confined to the positive attachments made. The necessity for a system of selection is largely due to the necessity for rejection. The good and great intimacies of our life may come to us as the wind blows, but by regulating our course wisely we will escape from hampering our life by mistakes and weakening it with false connections. We ought to be courteous and kind and gentle with all, but we cannot open the sanctuary of our heart to all.

We have a graduated scale of intimacy, from introduction, nodding acquaintance, and speaking acquaintance through an endless series of kinds of interchange to the perfect friendship. In counting up our gains and our resources, we cannot give them all the same value without deceiving ourselves. To expect loyalty and devotion from all alike is to court disappointment.

Most misanthropical and cynical estimates of man are due to this mingled ignorance and conceit. We cannot look for undying affection from the crowd we happen to have entertained at dinner or have rubbed shoulders with at business resorts or social gatherings. Many men in life (as often depicted in literature) have played the misanthrope because they have discovered through adversity how many of their associates were fair-weather friends. In their prosperity they encouraged obsequious flattery. They liked to have hangers-on who would flatter, but when the east wind blew they were indignant that their circle of friends preferred to avoid it.

Shakespeare's Timon of Athens is a typical misanthrope in his virtuous indignation at the love of men for comfort. In his prosperity, crowds of glass-faced flatterers bent before him and were made rich in Timon's nod. He wasted his substance in presents and hospitality, and bred a race of parasites and fair-weather friends. When he spent all and began to be in want, no man gave unto him. The winter shower drove away the summer flies. He had loved the reputation for splendid liberality and lavish generosity. He had sought to be a little god among men, bestowing favors and receiving homage, all of which was only a subtle form of selfishness.

*We sometimes drift into our
connections with people, but the
art of seamanship is tested by
sailing and not by drifting.*

When the brief day of prosperity passed, men shut their doors against the setting sun. The smooth and smiling crowd dropped off with a shrug, and Timon went to the other extreme, that of misanthropy, railing against friendship and cursing men for their ingratitude. But after all he got what he paid for. He thought he had been buying the hearts of men but found that he had only bought their mouths and tongues and eyes.

"He that loves to be flattered is worthy of the flatterer." For moral value there is not much to choose between them. Rats are said to desert the sinking ship, which is not to be wondered at in rats. The choice of friendship does not mean the indiscriminate acceptance of all who are willing to assume the name of friend. A touch of east wind is good, not only to weed out the false and test the true, but also to brace man to the stern realities of life. When we find that some of our intimates are dispersed by adversity, instead of raving against the world's ingratitude like Timon, we should be glad that now we know exactly whom we can trust.

Another common way of choosing friends, and one which also meets with its own fitting reward, is the selfish method of valuing men according to their usefulness to us. To add to their reputation, some people are willing to include anybody in their list of intimates. For business purposes men will sometimes run risks by endangering the peace of their home and the highest interests of those they love; they are ready to introduce into their family circle men whom they distrust morally, because they think they can make some gain out of the connection.

Much snobbery is due to the desire to make use of people in some way or other. It is an abuse of the word "friendship" to apply it to such social scrambling. Of course, even snobbery may be only a perverted desire after what we think the best, a longing to get near those we consider of nobler nature and larger mind than common associates. It may be an instinctive agreement with Plato's definition of the wise man as ever wanting to be with him who is better than himself. But in its usual form it becomes an unspeakable degradation, inducing servility, obsequiousness, and all the vices of the servile mind.

There can never be true friendship unless there is self-respect and unless soul meets soul free from self-seeking. If we had higher standards for ourselves, if we lived to God and not to men, we would find that in the truest sense we would live with men. We need not go out of our way to ingratiate ourselves with anybody. Nothing can make up for the loss of independence and native dignity of soul. It is not for a man, made in the image of God, to grovel and demean himself before his fellow creatures.

After all it defeats itself, for there can only be friendship *between equals*. This does not mean equals in what is called social position, or even in intellectual attainments, but it means equality which has a spiritual source. Can two walk together unless they be agreed? Nor does it mean identity, nor even likeness. Indeed, for the highest unity there must be *difference*, the difference of free beings with will and conscience and mind unhampered. We often make much of our differences, forgetting that we really differ, and *can* differ, only because we agree. Without many points of contact there could be no divergence from these. Argument and contradiction of opinion are the outcome of difference, and yet for argument there is needed a common basis. We cannot even discuss unless we meet on some mental ground common to both disputants.

For the highest union there must be a great general conformity behind the distinctions, a deep underlying common basis beneath the unlikeness. And for true union of hearts this equality must have a spiritual source. If there must be some spiritual affinity, agreement in what is best and highest in each, we can see the futility of most of the selfish attempts to make capital out of our interchanges. Our friends will be, because they must be, our equals. We can never have a nobler intimacy until we are made fit for it.

All connections based on selfishness, either on personal pleasure or on usefulness, are accidental. They are easily dissolved because, when the pleasure or the utility ceases, the bond ceases. When the motive of the friendship is removed, the friendship itself disappears. The perfect friendship is grounded on what is permanent—on goodness, on character. It is of much slower growth, since it takes some time to really find out the truly lovable things in a life, but it is lasting, since the foundation is stable.

The most important point about the choice of friendship is that we should know what to reject. Countless attractions come to us on the lower plane. A man may be attracted by what his own conscience tells him to be unworthy. He may have slipped gradually into companionship with people whose influence is evil and is deteriorating his life and character. He knows the fruits of his weakness in the lowering of his moral tone and in the slackening grip of his conscience. He has become pliant in will, feeble in purpose, and flaccid in character. Every man has a duty to be his own best self, and to do so he can never be under the spell of evil companionship.

Some men mix in doubtful company, and excuse it by saying that they have no Pharisaic exclusiveness. They sometimes even defend themselves by Christ's example, who received sinners and ate with them. The comparison borders on blasphemy. *It depends on the purpose for which sinners are received.* Christ never joined in their sin, but went to save them from their sin; wickedness could not lift its head in His presence.

Some seek to be initiated into the mysteries of iniquity in idle or morbid curiosity, perhaps to write a realistic book or to "see life" as it is called. There is often a prurient desire to explore the territory of sin, as if information on such subjects meant wisdom. If men are honest with themselves, they will admit that they join the company of sinners for the relish they have for the sin. We must obey the moral command to come out from among them and be separate before it is possible for us to meet them like Christ. Separateness of soul is the law of holiness. Of Christ, of whom it was said that this man receiveth sinners, it was also said that He was separate from sinners.

The knowledge of wickedness is not wisdom, nor is the counsel of sinners prudence. Most young men know the temptation here referred to, the curiosity to learn the hidden things and to have the air of those who know the world.

If we have gone wrong here, and have admitted into the sanctuary of our lives influences that make for evil, we must break away from them at all costs. The sweeter and truer relationships of our life should arm us for the struggle: the prayers of a mother, the sorrow of true friends. This is often the fear in the hearts of the folks at home when their boy leaves them to win his way in the city, the deadly fear that he may fall into evil habits and into the clutches of evil men. They know that there are men whose touch, whose words, whose very look, is contamination. To give them entrance into our lives is to submit ourselves to the contagion of sin.

Friends should be chosen by a higher principle of selection than any worldly one, whether of pleasure, or of usefulness, or of weak submission to the evil influences of our lot. Friends should be chosen for character, for goodness, for truth and trustworthiness, because they have sympathy with us in our

*Things arrange themselves
without effort, and by some
subtle affinity we learn that
we have gained a friend.*

best thoughts and holiest aspirations, because they have community of mind in the things of the soul. All other connections are fleeting and imperfect.

A relationship based on the physical withers when the first bloom fades, and a relationship founded on the intellectual is only a little more secure, as it too is subject to caprice. All purely earthly partnerships, like all earthly treasures, are exposed to decay, the bite of the moth, and the stain of the rust; they all have an end.

A young man may get opposing advice from two equally trusted counselors. One will advise him to cultivate the friendship of the clever, because they will afterward occupy places of power in the world; the other will advise him to cultivate the friendship of the good, because if they do not inherit the earth, they aspire to the heavens. If he knows the character of the two counselors, he will understand why they look upon life from such different standpoints, and later on he will find that while some of his friends were both clever and good, not one of the purely intellectual friendships remains to him. These do not afford a sufficient basis of agreement to stand the tear and wear of life. The basis of friendship must be community of soul.

The only permanent severance of heart comes through lack of a common spiritual footing. If one soul goes up the mountaintop and the other stays down among the shadows, if the two have not the same high thoughts and pure desires and ideals of service, they cannot remain together except in form. Friends need not be identical in temperament and capacity, but they must be alike in sympathy. An unequal yoke either becomes an intolerable burden or else will drag one of the partners away from the path that his soul at its best would have loved to tread.

If we choose our friends in Christ, neither now nor ever need we fear parting. We will have the secure joy and peace which come from having a friend who is as one's own soul.

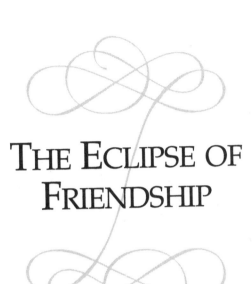

CHAPTER FIVE

THE ECLIPSE OF
FRIENDSHIP

The Eclipse of Friendship

As it is one of the greatest joys of life when a kindred soul is for the first time recognized and claimed, so it is one of the bitterest moments of life when the first rupture is made of the ties which bind us to other lives. Before it comes, it is hard to believe that it is possible, if we ever think of it at all. When it does come, it is harder still to understand the meaning of the blow. The miracle of friendship seemed too beautiful to carry in its bosom the menace of its loss. We knew, of course, that such things had been, and must be, but we never quite realized what it would be like to be the victims of such a loss.

If it only came as a sudden pain that passes

after its brief spasm of agony, it would not be so severe an affliction; but when it comes, it comes to stay. There remains a place in our hearts which is tender to every touch, and it is touched often. We survive the shock of the moment easier than the constant reminder of our loss. The old familiar face, now barred to our sense of sight, can be recalled by a stray word, a casual sight, a chance memory. The closer our fellowship had been, the more things in our lives are still associated with him—things we did together, places we visited together, even thoughts we thought together.

There seems to be no area of life where we can escape from the suggestions of memory. The sight of any little object can bring our former friend back, with his way of speaking, with his special gestures, with all the qualities for which we loved him and for which we now mourn him.

If the friendship was due to mere physical proximity, the loss will be only a vague sense of uneasiness through the breakdown of long-continued habit, but if the two lives were woven into the same web there must be ragged edges left, and it is a weary task to take up the threads again and find a new woof for the warp. The closer the connection has been, the keener the loss. It comes back to us at the sight of the many things associated with him, and try as we may to fill up our lives with countless distractions, the shadow creeps back to darken our world.

Sometimes there is the added pain of remorse that we did not adequately appreciate the treasure we possessed. In thoughtlessness we accepted the gift: We had so little idea of the true value of his friendship. We loved so little and were so impatient—if only we had him back again! If only we had one more opportunity to show him how dear he was, one more chance of proving ourselves worthy! We can hardly forgive ourselves that we were so cold and selfish. Self-reproach, the regret of the unaccepted opportunity, is one of the commonest feelings after bereavement, and it is one of the most blessed.

Still, it may become a morbid feeling. It is a false sentimentalism which lives in the past and lavishes its tenderness on memory. It is difficult to distinguish the dividing line between healthy sorrow and morbid sentiment. Sorrow seems a natural instinct, one which makes the bereaved care lovingly for the grave and the mother keep tenderly the little shoes worn by the little feet. But the instinct turns morbid when it preserves the room of a dead mother, with its petty decorations and ornaments as she left them. Beautiful as the instinct may be, there is nothing so dangerous as when our most natural feeling turns morbid.

It is always a temptation, which grows stronger the longer we live, to look back instead of forward, to bemoan the past, to deride the present and distrust the future. We must not forget our present blessings: the love we still possess, the gracious influences that remain, and most of all the duties that claim our strength. The loving women who went early in the morning to the sepulcher of the buried Christ were met with a rebuke: "Why seek ye the living among the dead?" They were sent back to life to find Him, and sent back to life to do honor to His death. Not by ointments and spices, nor at the rock-hewn tomb, could they best remember their Lord, but out in the world and in their lives.

Christianity does not condemn any natural human feeling, but it will not let these interfere with present duty and destroy future usefulness. It does not send people to search for the purpose of living in the graves of their dead hopes and pleasures. Its disciples must not attempt to live on the relics of great incidents, among crucifixes and tombs. In the desert of life the heart must reach forward to the Promised Land, and not back to Egypt.

The Christian faith is for the future because it believes in the God of the future. The world is not a lumber room, full of relics and remembrances, over which to brood. We are asked to remember the beautiful past which was ours, and the beautiful friends which have passed on, by making the *present* beautiful like it, and our lives beautiful like theirs.

It is human to think that life has no future if it now seems dark with griefs and graves. It comes as a shock to find that we must bury our sorrow and come into contact with the hard world again, living our common life once more.

The Christian learns to do this not because he has a short memory, but because he has a long faith. The voice of inspiration is heard oftener through the realities of life than through vain regrets and reclusive dreams. The Christian life must be like the Master's own life: luminous with His hope and surrounded by a bracing atmosphere which uplifts all who touch its outer fringe.

Yet the great fact of life is death, and it must have a purpose to serve and a lesson to teach. It seems to lose something of its impressiveness because it is so universal. The very inevitableness of it seems to kill thought rather than induce it. It is only when the blow strikes home that we are pulled up and forced to face the fact. Theoretically there is a wonderful unanimity among men regarding the shortness of life and the uncertainty of all human relationships. The last word of the wise on life has always been its fleetingness, its appalling changes, its unexpected surprises.

The only certainty of life is its uncertainty—its unstable tenure, its inevitable end. But practically we go on as if we could lay our plans and mortgage time without doubt or danger—until our feet are knocked out from under us by some sudden shock, and we realize how unstable the equilibrium of life really is. The lesson of life is death.

The experience would not be so tragically universal if it did not have a good and necessary meaning. For one thing, it should sober us and make our lives full of serious, solemn purpose. It should teach us to number our days that we may apply our hearts to wisdom. The man who has no place for death in his philosophy has not learned to live. The lesson of death is life.

Yet on the whole, it is not our own liability to death which oppresses us. The fear of it to a brave man, not to speak of a man of faith, can be overcome. It is the fear of it *for others whom we love* which is its sting. And not one of us can live very long without knowing in our own heart's experience the reality and terror of death. This too has its meaning for us: to look at life more tenderly and to touch it more gently. The pathos of life is only a forced sentiment to us if we have not felt the pity of life.

To a sensitive soul, smarting with his own loss, the world sometimes seems full of graves, and for a time this makes him walk softly among men.

This is one reason why making new friends is so much easier in youth than later on. Friendship comes to youth seemingly without any conditions and without any fears. There is no past to look back at with its regrets and sorrows. We never look behind us, *until we miss something*. Youth is satisfied with the joy of present possession. To the young friendship comes as the glory of spring, a miracle of beauty, a mystery of birth; to the old it has the bloom of autumn, still beautiful but with the beauty of decay. To the young it is chiefly hope; to the old it is mostly memory. The man who is conscious that he has lost the best of his days, the best of his powers, and the best of his friends naturally lives a good deal in the past.

Such a man is prepared for further losses; he has adjusted himself to the fact of death. At first we cannot believe that it can happen to us and to our love. Even if the thought comes to us, it is an event too far in the future to ruffle the calm surface of our heart. And yet it must come; none of us can escape it. Most of us can remember a night of waiting, too stricken for prayer, too numb of heart even for feeling, vaguely expecting the blow to strike us out of the dark. A strange sense of the unreality of things came over us as the black wave submerged us and passed on. We went out into the sunshine, and it seemed to mock us. We entered again among the busy ways of men, and the roar of life beat upon our brain and heart.

Was it worthwhile to have linked our lives to other lives and laid ourselves open to such desolation? Would it not be better to go through the world without joining ourselves too closely to the fleeting bonds of other loves? Why deliberately add to our disabilities? But it is not a disability; rather, the great purpose of all our living is to learn love, even though we must experience the pains of love as well as its joys. To cut ourselves off from this part of the human experience would be to impoverish our lives and deprive ourselves of the culture of the heart. Whatever the risks to our happiness, we cannot stand apart from the lot of mankind without ceasing to be men in the only true sense.

It is not easy to solve the problem of sorrow. Indeed there is no solution to it at all unless the individual works out his own solution. Most attempts at a philosophy of sorrow just end in high-sounding words. Explanations which profess to cover all the ground are as futile as the ordinary blundering attempts at comfort, which only patch grief with proverbs. The sorrow of our hearts is not appreciably lessened by argument. Any kind of philosophy—any wordy explanation of the problem—is at best poor comfort. It is not the problem which brings the pain in the first place; it is the pain which brings the problem. The heart's bitterness is not allayed by an exposition of the doctrine of providence. The father whose little daughter lies dead at home is not to be appeased in his anguish by a nicely balanced system of thought.

All of life is an argument for death. We cannot persist long in the effort to live the

Christian life without feeling the need for death. The higher the aims and the truer the aspirations, the greater is the burden of living. Sooner or later we are forced to make the confession of Job, "I would not live alway." To live forever in this sordidness, to have no reprieve from the doom of sin, no truce from the struggle of sin, would be a fearful fate.

To the Christian, therefore, death cannot be looked on as evil. Death is universal, and it is universal because it is God-ordained. In St. Peter's, at Rome, are many tombs in which death is symbolized in its traditional form as a skeleton, with the fateful hourglass and the fearful scythe. Death is the rude reaper who cruelly cuts off life and all the joy of life. But there is one tomb in which death is sculptured as a sweet, gentle, motherly woman who takes her wearied child home to safer and surer keeping. It is a truer thought than the other. Death is a minister of God, doing His pleasure and doing us good.

Death cannot be evil because it means a fuller life, and therefore an opportunity for fuller and further service. Faith will not let a

The world is not a
lumber room, full of relics
and remembrances, over which
to brood. We are asked to remember the beautiful past which
was ours, and the beautiful
friends which have passed on,
by making the <u>present</u> beautiful
like it, and our lives beautiful
like theirs.

man hasten the climax, for it is in the hands of love, as he himself is. But death is the climax of life. For if all of life is an argument for death, then all death is an argument for life.

Jowett says in one of his letters, "I cannot sympathize in all the grounds of consolation that are sometimes offered on these melancholy occasions, but there are two things which have always seemed to me unchangeable: first, that the dead are in the hands of God, who can do for them more than we can ask or have; and secondly, with respect to ourselves, that such losses deepen our views of life, and make us feel that we would not always be here." There are two noble grounds of consolation, and they are enough.

Death is the great argument for immortality. We cannot believe that the living, loving soul has ceased to be. We cannot believe that all those treasures of mind and heart are squandered in empty air. We will not believe it. When once we understand the meaning of the spiritual, we see the absolute certainty of eternal life; we need no arguments for the persistence of being.

To appear for a little time and then vanish away is the outward biography of all men: a circle of smoke that breaks, a bubble on the stream that bursts, a spark put out by a breath.

But there is another biography, a deeper and a permanent one: the biography of the soul. Everything that *appears* vanishes away; that is its fate, the fate of the everlasting hills as well as of the vapor that caps them. But that which does not appear, the spiritual and unseen, which we in our folly sometimes doubt because it does not appear, is the only reality; it is eternal and does not pass away. The material is only the garb of the spiritual, as speech is the clothing of thought. With our earthly standards we often think of the thought as the unsubstantial and the speech as the real. But speech dies upon the passing wind; the thought alone remains. We consider the sound to be the music, whereas it is only the expression of the music, and vanishes away.

Behind the material world, which waxes old as a garment, there is an eternal principle— the thought of God it represents. Above the sounds there is the music that can never die.

Beneath our lives, which vanish away, there is a vital thing—spirit. We cannot locate it and put our finger on it; that is why it is permanent. The things we can put our finger on are the things which appear, and therefore which fade and die.

Death to the spiritual mind is only *eclipse*. When there is an eclipse of the sun it does not mean that the sun is blotted out of the heavens; it only means that there is a temporary obstruction between it and us. If we wait a little, it passes. Love cannot die. Its forms may change, and even its objects, but its life is the life of the universe. It is not death, but sleep; not loss, but eclipse. The love is only transfigured into something more heavenly than ever before. Happy it is to have friends on earth, but happier still to have friends in heaven.

And it need not be even eclipse, except in outward form. Communion with the unseen can mean true correspondence with all we have loved and lost, if only our souls were responsive. The highest love is not starved by the absence of its object; it rather becomes more tender and spiritual, with more of the

THE ECLIPSE OF FRIENDSHIP

ideal in it. Ordinary affection, on a lower plane and dependent on physical attraction or on the earthly side of life, naturally crumbles to dust when its foundation is removed. But love is independent of time or space, and as a matter of fact is purified and intensified by absence. Separation of friends is not a physical thing. Lives can be sundered as if divided by infinite distance even though materially they are near each other. This tragedy is often enough enacted in our midst.

The converse is also true: Friendship does not really lose by death; it lays up treasure in heaven and leaves the very earth a sacred place, made holy by happy memories. Spiritual communion cannot be interrupted by a physical change. It is because there is so little of the spiritual in our ordinary fellowship that death means silence and an end to communion.

Love is the only permanent relationship among men, and the permanence is not an accident of it but is of its very essence. When released from the mere magnetism of sense, instead of ceasing to exist, it only then truly comes into its largest life. If our life were more a life in the spirit, we would be sure that death can be at its worst but the eclipse of friendship. Tennyson felt this truth in his own experience, and expressed it in noble form again and again in *In Memoriam*:

> *Sweet human hand and lips and eye,*
> *Dear heavenly friend that canst not die;*
>
> *Strange friend, past, present, and to be;*
> *Loved deeplier, darklier understood;*
> *Behold I dream a dream of good,*
> *And mingle all the world with thee.*
>
> *Thy voice is on the rolling air;*
> *I hear thee where the waters run;*
> *Thou standest in the rising sun,*
> *And in the setting thou art fair.*

It is not loss but momentary eclipse, and the final issue is a clearer perception of immortal love and a deeper consciousness of eternal life.

The attitude of mind in any such bereavement cannot be merely an attitude of resignation. The eclipse of love makes the love fairer when the eclipse passes. The loss of the outward purifies the affection and softens the heart. It brings out into fact what was often only latent in feeling. Memory adds a tender glory to the past. We only think of the *virtues* of the dead; we forget their faults. This is as it should be. We rightly love the immortal part of them; the fire has burned up the dross and left pure gold.

True sentiment does not weaken, but becomes an inspiration to make our life worthy of our love. However poor we may be in the world's goods, we are rich in happy associations in the past, and in sweet communion in the present, and in blessed hope for the future.

THE WRECK OF
FRIENDSHIP

CHAPTER SIX

The Wreck
of Friendship

The eclipse of friendship through death is not nearly so sad as the many ways in which friendship may be wrecked. There are worse losses than the losses of death, and to bury a friendship is a keener grief than to bury a friend. The latter softens the heart and sweetens the life, while the former hardens and embitters. The Persian poet Hafiz says, "Thou learnest no secret until thou knowest friendship, since to the unloving no heavenly knowledge enters."

But so imperfect are our human relationships that many a man has felt that he has bought his knowledge too dearly. Few of us go through the world without some scars on the heart, which even yet throb when the finger of memory touches them. In spite of all that has been said and may be said in praise of this golden friendship, it has too often been found how vain is the help of man. The deepest tragedies of life have been the failure of this very relationship.

In one way or other the loss of friendship comes to all. The shores of life are strewn with wrecks. The convoy which left the harbor confidently in the sunshine cannot all expect to arrive together in the haven. There is the danger of storms and collisions and of the separation of the night. Even at best, if accidents never occur, the whole company cannot all keep up with the speed of the swiftest.

There is a certain pathos in all loss, but there is not always pain in it, or at least it is of varied quality and extent. Some losses are natural and unavoidable, quite beyond our control, the result of resistless change. Some loss is even the necessary accompaniment of gain. The loss of youth with all its possessions is the gain of manhood and womanhood. A man must put away childish things, the speech and understanding and thought of a child. So the loss of some friendship comes as a part of the natural course of things, and is accepted without mutilating our life.

Many of our connections with people are admittedly casual and temporary. They exist for mutual convenience through common interest at the time, or common purpose, or common business. None of the partners asks for more than the advantage that each derives from the connection. When it comes to an end, we let the cable slip easily, and say good-bye with a cheery wave. With many people we meet and part in all friendliness and good feeling, and will be glad to meet again, but the parting does not tear at our affections. When the business is transacted the tie is loosed, and we each go our separate ways without much regret.

At other times there is no thought of gain, except the mutual advantage of conversation or companionship. We are pleasant to each other and enjoy the interchange of kindred tastes. Most of us have some pleasant recollections of happy meetings with interesting people, perhaps on holiday times, when we felt we would be glad to meet them again sometime. But even if we never saw them again, we do not feel much poorer for the loss.

We also *grow* out of some of our friendships. This is to be expected, since so many of them are formed thoughtlessly, or before we really knew either ourselves or our friends. They never meant very much to us. Most boyish friendships do not last long because they are not based on the qualities which wear well. Schoolboy comradeships are usually due to proximity rather than to character. They are the fruit of accident rather than of affinity of soul. Boys grow out of these as they grow out of their clothes. Now and again they suffer from growing pains, but it is more discomfort than anything else.

It is sad to look back and realize how few of our early companionships remain, but it is not possible to blame either party for the loss. Distance, separation of interest, and difference of work all operate to divide us. When athletics seemed the purpose of existence, friendship was based on football and baseball.

But as life opens out, other standards are set up, and a new principle of selection takes its place. When the world is seen to be more than a ball field, when it is recognized to be a stage on which men play many parts, a new kind of intimacy is demanded which is often not with the same persons. This kind of loss is the condition which accompanies true growth.

There is more chance for the permanence of friendships formed a little later. It must not be too long after this period, however, for when the generous time of youth has passed, it becomes hard to make new connections. People get overburdened with cares and personal concerns, and grow cautious about making advances.

In youth the heart is responsive and ready to be generous; the hand aches for the grasp of a comrade's hand, and the mind demands fellowship in the great thoughts that are beginning to dawn upon it. The closest friendships are formed early in life because we are less cautious; more open to impressions, and readier to welcome self-revelations. After middle life a man does not find it easy to give himself away, and keeps a firmer hand on his feelings. Whatever the faults of youth, it is usually unworldly in its estimates and uncalculating in its thoughts of the future.

The danger to such friendship is the danger of just letting it lapse. As life spreads out before our eager feet, new interests crop up, new relations are formed, and the old ties get worn away. We may believe the advice about not forsaking an old friend because the new is not comparable to him, but we can neglect the friendship by merely letting things slip past.

It is easier for some temperaments to make friends, and it is easier for some dispositions to keep them. Little faults of manner, little occasions of thoughtlessness, and lack of the little courtesies do more to separate people than glaring mistakes. There are some people so built that it is difficult to remain on very close terms with them because there are so many corners to knock against. Even strength of character, if unmodified by sweetness of disposition, adds to the difficulty of pulling together. Strong will can so easily develop into self-will, and decision can become dog-matism. Wit, the salt of conversation, loses its savor when it becomes ill-natured; a faculty for argument is in danger of becoming mere quarrelsomeness.

The ordinary amenities of life must be preserved among friends. We can never feel very safe with the person whose humor tends to bitter speaking or keen sarcasm, or with the person who flares up into hasty speech at every or no provocation, or with the person who is argumentative and assertive —

Who'd rather on a gibbet dangle
Than miss his dear delight to wrangle.

There are more breaches of the peace among friends through sins of speech than from any other cause. We do not treat our friends with enough respect. We make the vulgar mistake of looking upon the common as if it were therefore cheap in nature. We ought rather to treat our friend with a sort of sacred familiarity, as if we appreciated the precious gift that his friendship truly is.

Every change in a man's life brings a risk

We cannot expect the pleasure
of friendship without the duty,
the privilege without the
responsibility. We cannot
break off the threads of the web,
and then, when the mood is on
us, continue as though nothing
had happened. If such a
breakage has occurred, we
must go back and patiently join
the threads together again.

of letting go something of the past which it is a loss to part with. A change of work, or a change of residence, or entrance into a larger sphere brings a certain engrossment which leads to neglect of the richest friendship in the past life.

Friendship may lapse through the *misfortune of distance*. Absence does not always make the heart grow fonder. It only does so when the heart is securely fixed, and when it is a heart worth fixing. More often the other proverb is truer: Out of sight, out of mind. It is so easy for a man to become self-centered, and to impoverish his affections through sheer neglect. Ties once close get frayed and strained till they break, and we discover that we have said farewell to the past. Some kind of interchange is needed to maintain friendship.

Or friendship may lapse through the *fault of silence*. The misfortune of distance may be overcome by love, but the fault of silence crushes out feeling as the falling rain kills the kindled flame. Even the estrangements and misunderstandings which arise to all cannot long remain where there is a frank and candid interchange of thought. Hearts grow cold toward each other through neglect. There is a suggestive word from the old Scandinavian *Edda*: "Go often to the house of thy friend, for weeds soon choke up the unused path." It is hard to overcome the alienation caused by neglect, for there grows up a sense of resentment and injured feeling.

Among the petty things which wreck friendships, none is so common and so unworthy as money. It is a common cynical remark that the way to lose a friend is to lend him money. There is nothing which seems to affect the mind more and heart more than money. There seems a curse in it sometimes, so potent is it for mischief. Poverty, if it is too oppressive, may hurt the heart-life, but oftener it only reveals what true treasures there are in the wealth of the affections. Many of the disputes which separate brethren are about the dividing of the inheritance, and it seems that few friendships can survive the test of money.

Neither a borrower, nor a lender be,
For loan oft loses both itself and friend.

There must be something wrong with a friendship which breaks down so easily. It ought to be able to stand a severer strain than that. But the inner reason of the failure is often that there has been a moral degeneracy going on, a weakening of the fiber of character on one side or on both sides. The particular dispute, whether it be about money or about anything else, is only the occasion which reveals the slackening of the morale. The self-respect of the friend who asks the favor may have been damaged through a series of importunities, or there may have been a growing hardness of heart and selfishness in the friend who refuses the request. Otherwise, if two are on terms of communion, it is hard to see why the giving or receiving of this service should be any more unworthy than any other help which friends can grant to each other. True commerce of the heart should make all other necessary commerce possible. Communion includes sharing. To have things in common does not seem difficult when there is love in common.

Friendship has also been wrecked by outside means, by the evil of other people in evil speaking or in envy or in whispering tongues that delight in scandal. Some mean natures rejoice in sowing discord, carrying tales with just the slightest turn of a phrase or even a tone of the voice and giving a sinister meaning to an innocent word or act. Frankness can always prevent this from permanently wrecking friendship. Besides, we should judge no one, and certainly not a trusted friend, by a report of an incident or a hasty word. We should judge our friend by his record, by what we know of his character. When anything inconsistent with that character comes to our notice, it is only justice to him to at least suspend judgment, and it would be wisdom to refuse to credit it at all.

We sometimes wonder at finding a friend cold and distant to us, and perhaps we moralize on the fickleness and inconsistency of men, but the reason may be in ourselves. We cannot expect the pleasure of friendship without the duty, the privilege without the responsibility. We cannot break off the threads of the web, and then, when the mood is on us, continue as though nothing had happened. If such a breakage has occurred, we must go back and patiently join the threads together again.

Thoughtlessness has done more harm in this respect than ill-will. If we have lost a friend through selfish neglect, the loss is ours, and we cannot expect to take up the story where we left off years ago. There is a serene impudence about the treatment some people mete out to their friends, dropping them whenever it suits and thinking to take them up again when it happens to suit once more. We cannot expect to walk with another person when we have gone for miles along a different way. We will have to go back and befriend him again. If the fault has been ours, desire and shame should give wings to our feet.

The real source of separation is ultimately a spiritual one. We cannot walk with another person unless we are both agreed. The lapse of friendship is often due to the fact that one party has let the other travel on alone. Perhaps one has sought pleasure and the other truth; perhaps one has cumbered his life with the trivial and the petty while the other has filled his life with high thoughts and noble aspirations. If their hearts are on different levels, it is natural that they should now be apart.

If we would keep our best friends, we must go with them in sympathy and be able to share their thoughts. In the letters of Dean Stanley there is one from Jowett to Stanley which brings out this necessity: "I earnestly hope that the friendship which commenced between us many years ago may be a blessing to last us through life. I feel that if it is to be so we must both go onward, otherwise the tear and wear of life, and the 'having travelled over each other's minds,' and a thousand accidents will be sufficient to break it off. I have often felt the inability to converse with you, but never for an instant the least alienation. There is no one who would not think me happy in having such a friend."

It is not so much the equal pace of the mind which is necessary as the equal pace of the spirit. We may think about a very brilliant friend that he will outstrip us and outgrow us. The fear is natural, but if there is spiritual oneness it is an unfounded fear.

> *Yet oft, when sundown skirts the moor,*
> *An inner trouble I behold,*
> *A spectral doubt which makes me cold,*
> *That I should be thy mate no more.*

Love is not dependent on intellect. The great bond of union is not that both parties are alike in mind, but that they are akin in soul. Mere intellect only divides people further than the ordinary natural and artificial distinctions that already exist. Endless instances of this disuniting influence are seen in the contempt of learning for ignorance, the derisive attitude which knowledge assumes toward simplicity.

It is love, not logic, which can unite men. Love is the one solvent to break down all barriers, and love has other grounds for its existence than merely intellectual ones. Even though similarity of taste is another bond and is perhaps necessary for the perfect friendship, it is not its foundation; and if the foundation is not undermined, there is no reason why

Failure of one friend often
leads to distrust of all friends.
This is the terrible responsibility
of friendship. We have more
than the happiness of our
friend in our power; we have
his faith.

difference of mental power should wreck the structure.

However it happens that friends are separated, it is always sad, for the loss of a friendship is the loss of an ideal. Sadder than the pathos of unmated hearts is the pathos of severed souls. It is always a pain to find a friend look on us with cold stranger's eyes, and to find ourselves dead of hopes of future intimacy. It is a pain even when we have nothing to blame ourselves with—in fact more than when we feel the fault is ours. It would not matter very much if it were not such a loss to both parties, for friendship is one of the appointed means of saving the life from worldliness and selfishness. It is the greatest education in the world, for it is education of the whole man, of the affections as well as the intellect. Nothing of worldly success can make up for the lack of it.

True friendship is also a moral preservative. It teaches something of the joy of service and the beauty of sacrifice. We cannot live an utterly useless life if we have to think and act for another person. Such friendship keeps love in the heart and God in the life.

The greatest and most irretrievable wreck of friendship is the result of a moral breakdown in one of the associates. Worse than the separation of the grave is the desolation of the heart by faithlessness. More separating than the gulf of death is the great gulf fixed between souls through deceit and shame. It is as the sin of Judas. Said the sorrowful psalmist who had known this experience, "Mine own familiar friend in whom I trusted, which did eat of my bread, hath lifted up his heel against me." Another psalmist sobs out the same lament: "It was not an enemy that reproached me— then I could have born it—but it was thou, a man mine equal, my guide and mine acquaintance. We took sweet counsel together, and walked into the house of God in company."

The loss of a friend by any of the common means is not so hard as to find a friend faithless. The trustful soul has often been disillusioned in this way. The rod has broken in the hand that leaned on it, and has left its red wound on the palm. There is an even deeper wound on the heart.

The result of such a breakdown of comradeship is often bitterness and cynical distrust of man. It is this experience which gives point to the sneer, "Defend me from my friends; I can defend myself from my enemies!" Such cynicism is like treason within the camp, against which no man can guard. It is a stab in the back, a cowardly assassination of the heart. Treachery like this usually means a sudden fall from the ideal for the deceived one, and the ideal can only be recovered, if at all, by a slow and toilsome ascent, foot by foot and step by step.

Failure of one friend often leads to distrust of all friends. This is the terrible responsibility of friendship. We have more than the happiness of our friend in our power; we have his faith. Most sneers at friendship begin with the expression of individual pain because a person has known the shock of the lifted heel. Distrust works havoc on our character, for it ends in unbelief of goodness itself. And distrust always meets with its own likeness, and is paid back in its own coin.

The social virtues which keep the whole

community together are closely allied to the supreme virtue of friendship. Aristotle had reason in making it the link between his ethics and his politics. Truth and good faith—honest dealing between man and man—is necessary for any kind of interchange, even that of business. Men can do nothing with each other if they do not have a certain minimum of trust. There have been times when there seems to be almost an epidemic of faithlessness, when the social bond seems loosened and when men's hands are raised against each other, when confidence is paralyzed and people hardly know whom to trust.

The prophet Micah, who lived in such a time, expressed this state of distrust: "Trust ye not any friend, put ye no confidence in a familiar friend. A man's enemies are of his own household." This means anarchy, and society becomes like a bundle of sticks with the cord cut. The cause is always a decay of religion, for law is based on morality, and morality finds its strongest sanction in religion. Selfishness results in anarchy, a reversion to the Ishmaelite type of life.

The story of the French Revolution has in it some of the darkest pages in the history of modern civilization, due to the breakdown of social trust. Suspicion during the reign of terror brooded over the heads of men and oppressed their hearts. The ties of blood and fellowship seemed broken, and the sad words of Christ had their horrible fulfillment in that brother delivered up brother to death.

There are some awful possibilities in human nature. In the Paris of those days a man had to be always on his guard, watching his acts, his words, even his looks. It meant for a time a collapse of the whole idea of the state. It was a panic, worse than avowed civil war. Friendship could have little place in such a frightful palsy of mutual confidence, though there were some noble exceptions. The wreck of friendship through deceit is always a step toward social anarchy, for it helps to break down trust and good faith among men.

The wreck of friendship is also a blow to religion. Many people have lost their faith in God because they have lost their faith in man. Doubt of the reality of love becomes doubt of the reality of spiritual life. To be unable to see the divine in man is to have the eyes blinded to the divine anywhere. Deception in the sphere of love shakes the foundation of religion. Its result is atheism, not perhaps as a conscious speculative system of thought, but as a subtle practical influence on conduct. It corrupts the fountain of life and taints the whole stream.

Despair of love, if final and complete, would be despair of God, for God is love. Thus the wreck of friendship often means a temporary wreck of faith. This danger should impress us with the deep responsibility attached to our friendships, for our life follows the fortunes of our love.

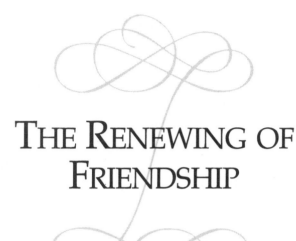

CHAPTER SEVEN

The Renewing of Friendship

The Renewing of Friendship

I t is a sentiment of the poets and romancers that love is often helped by quarrels. There must be some truth in this, as we find the idea expressed a hundred times in different forms of literature. We find it among the wisdom of the ancients, and it remains as one of the conventional properties of the dramatist and one of the accepted traditions of the novelist. It is expressed in maxim and play and poem.

It is the chief stock-in-trade of the writer of fiction to depict the misunderstandings which arise between two persons through the sin of one or the folly of both or the villainy of a third. Then come the means by which the tangled skein is unraveled, and in the end everything is satisfactorily explained and the sorely tried characters are ushered into a happiness stronger and sweeter than ever before. Friends quarrel and are miserable in their state of separation, but afterward, when the friendship is renewed, it is discovered that the bitter dispute was only a blessing in disguise, because the renewal itself was an exquisite pleasure, and the result is a firmer and more stable relationship of love and trust.

The truth in this sentiment is the evident one: that a man often wakens to the value of a possession only when he is in danger of losing it. The force of a current is sometimes noted only when it is opposed by an obstacle. Two persons may discover by a temporary alienation how much they really care for each other. It may be that previously they took things for granted. Their affection had lost its first glitter and was accepted as commonplace. Through some misunderstanding or dispute they broke off their friendly relationship, feeling sure that they had come to an end of their mutual regard.

They could never again be on the same close terms, for hot words had been spoken, taunts and reproaches had passed, eyes had flashed fire, and they had parted in anger—only to learn that their love for each other was as real and as strong as ever. The very difference revealed the true union of hearts that had existed. They had been blind to the strength of their mutual regard until it was so painfully brought to their notice. Then love was renewed with a more tender sense of its sacredness and a more profound feeling of its strength. The dissensions only displayed the union; the discord drove them to a fuller harmony. This is a natural and common experience.

But a mistake may easily be made by confusing cause and effect. "The course of true love never did run smooth," but the obstacles in the channel do not *produce* the swiftness and the volume of the stream; they only *show* them. An unsuspected depth and force may for the first time be brought to light when the stream strikes a barrier, but the barrier is merely the occasion and not the cause of the revelation. To mistake one for the other may *lead* to a false and foolish policy. Through this mistake many people act as though dissension were of the very nature of affection, and as if the one must necessarily react on the other for good. Some foolish people sometimes even produce disagreement for the supposed pleasure of agreeing once more, and quarrel for the sake of making it up again.

But the end of love is near at hand when wrangling can live in its presence. It is not true that love is helped by quarrels, except in the small sense already indicated. A man may quarrel once too often with his friend. A brother offended, says the proverb, is harder to be won than a strong city, and such contentions are like the bars of a castle. It is always a dangerous experiment to wilfully test affection. Disputing is a shock to confidence, and without confidence friendship cannot continue. A state of feud, even though a temporary one often embitters the life and leaves its mark on the heart.

Desolated homes and lonely lives are witnesses of the folly of such a policy. From the root of bitterness there cannot possibly blossom any of the fair flowers of love. We have acknowledged the surface truth of the poets' sentiment, but it is only a surface truth. The best of friends will fall out, and the best of them will renew their friendship, but it is always at great risk, and sometimes it sorely strains the foundations of their esteem for each other.

In any serious rupture of friendship it can only be a blessing when the tears of repentance flow. In all renewing there must be an element of repentance, and however great the joy of having regained the old footing, there is the memory of pain and the presence of regret. To cultivate contention as an art, and to trade upon the supposed benefit of renewing friendship, is a folly which brings its own retribution.

For this reason the contentious person never makes a good friend. In friendship men look for peace and harmony and some measure of contentment. There are enough battles to fight outside, enough disputing in the marketplace, enough discord in the workaday world without having to look for contention in the realm of the inner life also. There, if anywhere,

In friendship men look for
peace and harmony and some
measure of contentment. There
are enough battles to fight
outside, enough disputing in the
marketplace, enough discord in
the workaday world without
having to look for contention in
the realm of the inner life also.
There, if anywhere, we ask for
an end of strife. Friendship is
the sanctuary of the heart, and
the peace of the sanctuary
should brood over it.

we ask for an end of strife. Friendship is the sanctuary of the heart, and the peace of the sanctuary should brood over it. Its greatest glory is that the dust and noise of contest are excluded.

Of course it must be that offenses will come. It is not only that the world is full of conflict and controversy, and that every man must take his share in the fights of his time. We are born into the battle; indeed, we are born *for* the battle. But apart from the outside strife, from which we cannot separate ourselves (and do not desire to separate ourselves if we are true men), the strange thing is that offenses come inevitably even among brethren. The bitterest disputes in life are among those who are nearest each other in spirit.

We do not quarrel with the man in the street, the man with whom we have little or no communication. He has neither the chance nor the power to chafe our soul and ruffle our temper. If necessary we can afford to despise or at least neglect him. It is the man of our own household, near us in life and spirit, who runs the risk of the only serious dissensions with us. The man with whom we have most points of contact presents the greatest number of places where difference can occur. Only from circles that touch each other can a tangent strike off from the same point. A man can only make enemies among his friends. A man must be prepared for a certain amount of opposition and enmity in this world unless he lives a very sheltered life. But that two who have walked as friends, one in aim and one in heart, should speak as foes and not as lovers of the same love is, in spite of the poets and romancers, the bitterest moment of life.

There are some people we cannot hurt even if we would, whom all the venom of our nature could not touch because we mean nothing to them. But there are others in our power whom we can stab with a word, and these are our brethren, our familiar friends, our comrades at work, our close associates, our fellow laborers in God's vineyard. It is not the crowd that idly jostles us in the street that can hurt us to the quick, but a familiar friend in whom we trusted. He has a means of entry barred to strangers, and can strike home as no other can.

This explains why family quarrels and church disputes are so bitter: They come so near us. An offended brother is hard to win because the very closeness of the previous intimacy brings a rankling sense of injustice and the resentment of injured love. An injury from the hand of a friend seems such a wanton thing; the heart hardens itself with the sense of wrong, and a separation ensues like the bars of a castle.

The strife-makers find in themselves, in their barren heart and empty life, their own appropriate curse. The blow they strike comes back upon themselves. Worse than the choleric temperament is the peevish, sullen nature. The former usually finds a speedy repentance for its hot and hasty mood, but the other is a constant menace to friendship, and acts like a perpetual irritant. Its root is selfishness, and it grows by what it feeds on.

When offenses do come, we may use them as opportunities for growth in gracious ways, and thus turn them into blessings on the lives of both parties. To the offended it may be an occasion for patience and forgiveness, and to the offender an occasion for humility and frank confession. To both it may be a renewing of love less open to offense in the future. Christ's recipe for a quarrel among brethren is: "If thy brother shall trespass against thee, go and tell him his fault between thee and him alone; if he shall hear thee, thou hast gained thy brother."

Much of our dissension is due to misunderstanding, which could be put right by a few honest words and a little open dealing. Human beings so often live at cross purposes with each other when a frank word or a simple confession of wrong would heal the division. Resentment grows through brooding over a fancied slight. Hearts harden themselves in silence, and as time goes on it becomes more difficult to break through the silence.

Often there are strained relations among people who at the bottom of their hearts have sincere respect for each other, as well as smoldering affection which only needs a little coaxing of the spark to burst out again into a dancing flame. There is a terrible waste of human friendship, a waste of power which might be used to bless all our lives in our sinful separations, our selfish exclusiveness, our resentful pride.

We let the sweetest souls we have met die without acknowledging our debt to them. We stand aside in haughty isolation until the open grave opens our sealed hearts—too late. We let the chance of reconciliation pass till it is irrevocable. Most of us can remember a tender spot in the past somewhere, a sore place, a time when discord entered with another person we loved, and—

> *Each spake words of high disdain*
> *And insult to his heart's best brother.*

In some cases, as with the friends in Coleridge's great poem, the parting has been eternal, and neither party has ever since found another such friend to fill the life with comfort and free the hollow heart from hurting.

There is more damage from such a state of discord than the mere loss which it is to both parties; it influences the whole heart-life, creating bitterness, universal suspicion, or cynicism. Hatred is as contagious as love is.

They have an effect on the whole character, and are not confined to the single incident which causes the love or the hate. To hate a single one of God's creatures is to harden the heart to some extent against all.

Love is the center of a circle which broadens out in ever-widening circumference. Dante tells us in *La Vita Nuova* that the effect of his love for Beatrice was to open his heart to all, and to sweeten all his life. He speaks of the surpassing virtue of her very salutation to him in the street: "When she appeared in any place, it seemed to me, by the hope of her excellent salutation, that there was no man mine enemy any longer; and such warmth of charity came upon me that most certainly in that moment I would have pardoned whomsoever had done me an injury; and if any one should then have questioned me concerning any matter, I could only have said unto him 'Love,' with a countenance clothed in humbleness." His love bred sweetness in his mind, and took in everything within the blessed sweep of its range.

Hatred also is the center of a circle, one which has a baneful effect on the whole life.

We cannot have bitterness or resentment in our mind without its coloring our every thought and affection. Hatred toward one person will affect our attitude toward all people.

If we possess the spirit to be reconciled with an offended or an offending brother, there are some things which may be said about the tactics of renewing the broken tie. There is needed a certain tactful considerateness. In all such questions the grace of the act depends as much on the *manner* of it as on the act itself. The grace of the fairest act may be hurt by a boorish manner. Many a graceful act is spoiled by a graceless touch, even as a generous deed can be ruined by a grudging manner. An air of condescension will destroy the value of the finest act of charity. There is a forgiveness which is no forgiveness at all—formal, constrained, from the teeth and lips outward. It does not come as the warm breath which has had contact with the blood of the heart. The highest forgiveness is so full and free that it is forgetfulness. It is as complete as the forgiveness of God.

If there is something in the method of the

approach, there is even perhaps more in the timing of it. It ought to be chosen carefully and considerately, for it may be that the other person has not been as prepared for the renewal by thought and feeling as has the man who makes the advances. No hard-and-fast rule can be formulated when dealing with such a complex and varied subject because so much depends on temperament and character. One man taken by surprise reveals his true feeling, but another is irritated, and shuts up his heart in a sort of instinctive self-defense. The thoughtfulness of love will suggest the appropriate means, but some emphasis may rightly be given to the phrase in Christ's counsel, "between thee and him alone."

Let there be an opportunity for a frank and private conversation. To appeal to an estranged friend before witnesses induces to special pleading, making the witnesses the jury, asking for a verdict on either side. The result is that both are still convinced they have right on their side, and that they have been wronged.

If the fault of the estrangement lies with

us, the burden of confession should rest upon us also. To go to him with sincere penitence is no more than our duty. Whether the result is successful or not, it will mean a blessing for our own soul. Humility brings its own reward, for it brings God into our life. Even if we have cause to suspect that the offended brother will not receive us kindly, such reparation as we can make is at least the gate to reconciliation. It may be too late, but confession will lighten the burden on our own heart. If our brother is so offended that he is harder to be won than a strong city, he is far more worth winning. Even if the effort is unsuccessful, it is better than the cowardice which suffers a bloodless defeat.

If, on the other hand, the fault was not ours, our duty is still clear. It should be even easier to take the initiative in such a case, for it is much easier to forgive than to be forgiven. To some natures it is hard to be laid under an obligation, and the generosity of love must be shown by the offended brother. He must show the other his fault gently and generously, not parading his forgiveness like a virtue, but as if

It is sooner or later found
that the most perfect love cannot
utterly satisfy the heart of man.

A man must discover that there
is an infinite in him which only
the infinite can match
and supply.

the favor were on his side—as it is. Christ made forgiveness the test of spirituality. If we do not know the grace of forgiveness, we do not know how gracious life may be. The highest happiness is not a matter of possessions and material gains, but has its source in a heart at peace.

The renewing of friendship has a spiritual result. If we are revengeful, censorious, judging others harshly, always putting the worst construction on a word or an act, uncharitable, unforgiving, we certainly cannot claim kinship with the spirit of the Lord Jesus. The apostle Paul made the opposite the very test of the spiritual man: "Brethren, if a man be overtaken in a fault, ye which are spiritual restore such a one in the spirit of meekness."

If we knew all, we would forgive all. If we knew all the facts—the things which produced the petulance and the soreness which caused the irritation—we would be ready to pardon, for we would understand the temptation. If we knew all, our hearts would be full of love even for those who have wronged us. They have wronged themselves more than they can possibly wrong us; they have wounded a man to their own hurt. To think kindly once more of a separated friend, to soften the heart toward an offending brother, will bring the blessing of the Peacemaker, the blessing of the Reconciler. The way to be sure of acting this part is to pray for the brother. We cannot remain angry with another person when we pray for him. Offense departs when prayer comes. The captivity of Job was turned when he prayed for his friends.

If we stubbornly refuse the renewing of friendship, it is an offense against religion also. Only love can fulfill the law of Christ. His is the gospel of reconciliation, and the greater reconciliation includes the lesser. The friends of Christ must be friends of one another. That ought to be accepted as an axiom. To be reconciled to God carries with it a disposition of heart which makes it easy to be reconciled to men also. We have cause to suspect our religion if it does not make us gentle and forbearing and forgiving, if the love of our Lord does not so flood our hearts as to cleanse them of all bitterness and spite and wrath. If a man is nursing anger, if he is letting his mind become a nest of foul passions, malice, hatred, and evil wishing, how dwells the love of God in him?

If we cannot humble ourselves to win our brother, it is difficult to see where our religion comes in, especially when we think what humiliation Christ suffered that He might reconcile us to God and make us friends again with our heavenly Father, renewing our broken love. Whatever our faith and works, and however correct our creed and conduct, if we are giving place to anger, if we are stiffening ourselves in strife and disdain, we are none of His who was meek and lowly of heart. We may come to the Sanctuary with lips full of praises and eyes full of prayers, with devotion in our hearts and gifts in our hands, but God will spurn our worship and despise our gifts.

It is not a small matter, this renewing of friendship, but is the root of religion itself, and is well made the very test of spiritual-mindedness. "If thou bring thy gift to the altar, and there rememberest that thy brother hath aught against thee, leave there thy gift before the altar and go thy way; first be reconciled to thy brother, and then come and offer thy gift." Misunderstandings and estrangements will arise, and occasions will come when it seems as if not even love and forbearance can avoid a quarrel, but surely Christ has died in vain if His grace cannot save us from the continuance of strife.

Such renewing of love, done with this high motive, will indeed bring an added joy. The very pain will give zest to the pleasure. We will take the great gift of friendship with a new sense of its beauty and sacredness. We will walk more softly because of the experience, and more than ever will tremble lest we lose it. For days after the reconciliation we will go about with the feeling that the benediction of the peacemakers rests on our head and clings round our feet.

But more than any personal joy from the renewed friendship, we will have the smile of God on our life. We will know that we have done what is well-pleasing in His sight. Sweeter than the peace which comes from being at one with men is the peace which comes from being at one with God. It settles on the soul like the mist on the mountains, enveloping and enswathing it. It comes to our fevered life as a great calm. Over the broken waters hovers the golden glory of God's eternal peace.

And even more than all that, we will have gained a new insight into the love of the Father, and into the sacrifice of the Son. We will understand a little more of the mystery of the Love which became poor, which gladly went into the wilderness to seek and to save the lost. The cross will gain new and rich significance to us, and all the world will be an arena in which is enacted the spectacle of God's great love. The world is bathed in the love of God as it is flooded by the blessed sun. If we are in the light and walk in love, our walk will be with God, and His gentleness will make us great.

His intention for us is an ever-fuller education in the meaning and life of love, until the assurance reaches us that nothing can separate us from love. Even death, which sunders us from our friends, cannot permanently divide us. In the great homecoming and reunion of hearts, all the veils which obscure feeling will be torn down, and we shall know each other better and love each other more fully.

But every opportunity carries a penalty; every privilege brings with it a warning. If we will not live the life of love, if we harden our heart against a brother offended, we will find in our need even the great and infinite love of God shut against us, harder to be won than a strong city, ribbed and stockaded as the bars of a castle. To the unforgiving there is no forgiveness. To the hard and relentless, and loveless there is no love. To the selfish there is no heaven.

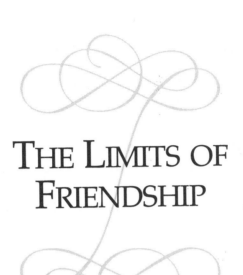

CHAPTER EIGHT

THE LIMITS OF
FRIENDSHIP

The Limits of Friendship

Friendship, even at its very best and purest, has limits. At its beginning it seems to have no conditions, and to be capable of endless development. In the first flush of newborn love it seems almost an insult to question its absolute power to meet every demand made upon it. The exquisite joy of understanding and being understood is too keen to let us believe that there may be a line beyond which we may not pass. Friendship comes as a mystery—formless, undefined, without set bounds. It is often a sad experience to discover that it is limited, like everything human. At first to speak of friendship as having qualifications was a profanation, and to find them out came as a disillusionment.

Yet the discovery is not all a loss. Whatever is limitless is also vague, and it is well to know the exact terms implied in a relationship. Of course we learn through experience the restrictions on all intimacy, and if we are wise we learn to keep well within the boundaries. Many a disappointment might have been saved if we had understood the inherent limitations of the subject. These are the result of personality. Each partner is after all a distinct individual, with will and conscience and life apart, with a personal responsibility which none can take from him, and with an individual bias of mind and heart which can never be ignored.

As is to be expected, some of the limits of friendship are not essential to the relation, but are due to a defect in the relationship, perhaps an idiosyncrasy of character or a peculiarity of temperament. Some of the limits are self-imposed, and arise from mistake or folly. A friend may be too exacting, and may make excessive demands, which strain the bond to the breaking point. There is often a good deal of selfishness in the affection, which asks for absorption and is jealous of other interests. Jealousy is usually the fruit not of love but of self-love.

Life is bigger than any relationship, and covers more ground. The circles of life may intersect, with part of each common to the other, but there will be an area on both sides exclusive to each. Even if it were possible for the circles to be concentric, it could hardly be that the circumference of the two would be the same: Almost without a doubt one would be of larger radius than the other. It is not *identity* which is the aim and the glory of friendship, but *unity in the midst of difference*. To strive at identity is to be certain of failure, and indeed deserves failure, for it is the outcome of selfishness. A man's friend is not his property, to be claimed as his exclusive possession. Jealousy is an ignoble vice because it has its roots in egotism. It also destroys affection because it is an evidence of lack of trust, and trust is essential to friendship.

There are physical limits to friendship, if nothing else. There are material barriers to be surmounted before human beings really get in touch with each other, even in the slightest degree. The physical senses are at best limited in their range and are always exposed to error. Flesh stands in the way of a complete revelation of soul. Human feet cannot enter past the threshold of the soul's abode. The very means of self-revelation is self-conceal-ment. Words obscure thought by the very process through which alone thought is pos-sible for us, and the fleshly wrappings of the soul hide it at the same time that they make it visible.

If there are physical limits to friendship, there are even greater mental limits. The needs of living press on us, and drive us into different currents of action. Our varied ex-perience colors all our thought and gives a special bias to our mind. There is a personal equation which must always be taken into ac-count. This is the charm of friendship but it is also a limitation. We do not travel over the same ground; we meet, but we also part.

However great the sympathy, it is not possible to completely enter into another man's mind, to look at a subject with his eyes. Much of our impatience with each other, and most of our misunderstandings, are caused by this natural limitation. The lines along which our minds travel can at best be asymptotic, approaching each other indefinitely near, but never quite coinciding.

The greatest limit of friendship, of which these others are but indications, is the spiritual fact of the separate personality of each human being. This is seen most absolutely in the sphere of morals. The ultimate standard for a man is his own individual conscience, and neither the constraint of affection nor the authority of numbers can atone for falseness there.

The influence of a friend or near relative is bound to be great. We are affected on every side, and at every moment, by the environment of other lives. There is a spiritual affinity, which is the closest and most powerful thing in the world, and yet in the realm of morals it has definite limits set to it. At best it can only go a certain length, and ought not to be allowed to go further than its legitimate bounds.

The most intimate of relatives, the most trusted of friends, must not be permitted to abrogate the place of conscience. Affection may be perverted into an instrument of evil. There is an even higher moral law than the law of friendship. The demands of friendship must not be allowed to interfere with the dictates of duty. It is not that the moral law should be obeyed blindly, but because in obeying it we are choosing the better part for both. Frederick Robertson says, "The man who prefers his dearest friend to the call of duty will soon show that he prefers himself to his dearest friend." Such weak giving in to the supposed higher demand of friendship is only a form of selfishness.

Friendship is sometimes too exacting. It asks for too much: more than we have to give, more than we ever ought to give. There is a tyranny of love, making demands which can only be granted to the loss of both parties. Such tyranny is a perversion of the nature of love, which is to serve, not to rule. It would override conscience and break down the will. We cannot give up our personal duty even as we cannot give up our personal responsibility. That is how it is possible for Christ to say that if a man love father or mother or wife more than Him, he is not worthy of Him. No human being can take the place of God to another life; it is blasphemy to attempt it.

There is a love which is evil in its selfishness. Its very exclusive claim is a sign of its evil root. The rights of the individual must not be renounced, even for love's sake. Human love can ask too much, and it asks too much when it would break down the individual will and conscience.

> *The hands that love us often are the hands*
> *That softly close our eyes*
>   *and draw us earthward.*
> *We give them all the largesse of our life—*
> *Not this, not all the world, contenteth them,*
> *Till we renounce our rights as living souls.*

We cannot renounce our rights as living souls without *losing* our souls. No man can pay the debt of life for us. No man can take the burden of life from us. To no man can we hand over the reins unreservedly. It would be

The lesson of all true living in every sphere is to learn our own limitations. It is the first lesson in art to work within the essential limitations of the particular art. But in dealing with other lives it is perhaps the hardest of all lessons to learn and submit to our limitations. It is the crowning grace of faith when we are willing to submit, and to leave those we love in the hands of God.

cowardice, and cowardice is sin.

The first axiom of the spiritual life is the sacredness of the individuality of each person. We must respect each other's personality. Even when we have rights over other people, these rights are strictly limited, and carry with them a corresponding duty to respect their rights also. The one intolerable despotism in the world is the attempt to put a yoke on the souls of men, and there are some forms of intimacy which approach that despotism. To transgress the moral bounds of friendship is to make the highest forms of friendship impossible, for these are reached only when free spirits meet in the unity of the spirit.

The community of human life is a great fact. We are all bound up in the same bundle. In a very true sense we stand or fall together. We are ever on our trail as a society, not only materially, but even in the highest things, morally and spiritually. There is a social conscience which we affect and which constantly affects us. We cannot rise very much above it, and fall much below it is for all true purposes

to cease to live. We have recognized social
standards which test morality; we have common ties, common duties, common responsi-
bilities.

But with it all, in spite of the fact of the
community of human life, there is the other
fact of the singleness of human life. We have a
life which we must live *alone*. We can never
get past the ultimate fact of personal responsibility. We may be leaves from the same tree of
life, but no two leaves are alike. We may be
wrapped up in the same bundle, but one bundle can contain very different things. Each of
us is colored with his own shade, separate
and peculiar. We have our own special powers
of intellect, our own special experience, our
own moral conscience, our own moral life to
live. So, while it is true that we stand or fall together, it is an even deeper truth that we stand
or fall alone.

In this crowded world, with its inter-
course and jostling, with its network of relationships, with its mingled web of life, we are
each alone. Below the surface there is a deep,
and below the deep there is a deeper depth.

In the depth of the human heart there is, and there must be, solitude. There is a limit to the possible communion with another person. We never completely open up our nature to even our nearest and dearest. In spite of ourselves something is kept back.

It is not that we are untrue in this, and hide our inner self, but simply that we are unable to reveal ourselves entirely. There is a bitterness of the heart which only the heart itself knows; there is a joy of the heart with which no stranger can meddle; there is a bound beyond which even a friend who is as our own soul becomes a stranger. There is a Holy of Holies over the threshold of which no human feet can pass. It is safe from trespass, guarded from intrusion, and even we ourselves cannot give to another person the key to open the door.

In spite of all the complexity of our social life, and the endless connections we form with other people, there is as the ultimate fact a great and strange solitude. We may fill up our hearts with human fellowship in all its grades, yet there remains to each person a distinct and separate life.

We speak vaguely of the mass of humanity, but the mass consists of units, each with his own life, a thing apart. The community of human life is being emphasized today, and it is a lesson which bears and needs repetition, the lesson of our common ties and common duties. But at the same time we dare not lose sight of the fact of the *singleness* of human life, because otherwise we have no moral appeal to make on behalf of those ties and duties.

In the region of morals, in dealing with sin, we see how true this solitude is. Even though there are truly social and national sins, and people can sin as a group, in its ultimate issue sin is *individual*. It is a disintegrating thing, separating a person from his fellowman and separating him from God. We are alone with our sin: in the final analysis there is nothing in the universe but God and the single human soul. People can share the sinning with us, but no one can share the sin. "The sin ye do by two and two, ye must pay for one by one." Therefore in this sphere of morals there must be limits to friendship, even with the friend who is as our own soul.

Friendship is a very real and close thing. It is one of the greatest joys in life, and has noble fruits. We can do much for each other: There are burdens we can share; we can rejoice with those who do rejoice and weep with those who weep. Through sympathy and love we are able to get out of self; and yet even here there are limits.

Our helplessness in the presence of grief proves this fundamental singleness of human life. When we stand beside a friend before the open grave, under the cloud of a great sorrow, we learn how little we can do for him. We can only stand speechless, and pray that the great Comforter may come with His own divine tenderness, and enter the sanctuary of sorrow shut to feet of flesh. Mourners have indeed been soothed by a touch, or a look, or a prayer, which had their source in a compassionate human heart, but it is only as a message of condolence flashed from one world to another. There is a burden which every man must bear, and none can bear for him; there is an aspect of our personality which we cannot unveil to human eyes. We must indeed live our own life and die our own death.

In the time of desolation, when the truth of this solitude is borne in on us, we are left to ourselves, not because our friends are unfeeling, but simply because they are unable. It is not their selfishness which keeps them off, but just their frailty. Their spirit may be willing, but the flesh is weak. It is a great lesson of life that there is no support in the arm of flesh, that even if there is no limit to human love, there is a limit to human power. Sooner or later it is the experience of every son of man, as it was the experience of the Son of Man, "Behold, the hour cometh, and now is come, that ye my friends shall be scattered every man to his own, and shall leave me alone."

Human friendship must have limits just because it is human. It is subject to loss and is often influenced by occasion. It lacks permanence: Misunderstandings can estrange us; slander can embitter us; death can bereave us. We are left very much the victims of circumstances, for, like everything earthly, friendship is open to change and decay. No matter how close and spiritual the fellowship, it is not permanent and never certain. If nothing else, the shadow of death is always on it. Tennyson describes how he dreamed that he and his friend should pass through the world together, loving and trusting each other, and together pass out into the silence.

> *Arrive at last the blessed goal,*
> *And He that died in Holy Land*
> *Would reach us out the shining hand,*
> *And take us as a single soul.*

It was a dream at best. Neither to live together nor to die together could blot out the spiritual limits of friendship. Even in the closest of human relations, when two take each other for better or for worse, for richer or for poorer, in sickness and in health, they may be made one flesh but never one soul. Singleness is the ultimate fact of human life. "The race is run by one and one, and never by two and two."

In the deepest things of the spirit, these limits we have been considering are perhaps felt most of all. Even with a friend who is as one's own soul, we cannot seek to make a spiritual impression without realizing the constraint of his separate individuality. We cannot break through the barriers of another person's distinct existence. If we have ever sought to lead to a higher life another person whom we love, we must have been made to realize that it does not all rest with us—that he is a free moral being, and that only by voluntarily yielding his heart and will and life to the King can he enter the kingdom. We are forced to respect his personality. We may watch and pray and speak, but we cannot save.

There is almost a sort of spiritual indecency in unveiling the naked soul, in attempting to invade the personality of another life. There is sometimes a spiritual vivisection which some people attempt in the name of religion, but which is actually immoral. Only holier eyes than ours, only more reverent hands than ours, can deal with the spirit of a man. He is a separate individual, with all the rights of an individual. We may have many points of contact with him (the contact of mind on mind and heart on heart), and we may even have rights over him (the rights of love), but he can at will insulate his life from ours. Here also, as elsewhere when we go deep enough into life, it is God and the single human soul.

The lesson of all true living in every sphere is to learn our own limitations. It is the first lesson in art to work within the essential limitations of the particular art. But in dealing with other lives it is perhaps the hardest of all lessons to learn and submit to our limitations. It is the crowning grace of faith when we are willing to submit, and to leave those we love in the hands of God. Nowhere else is the limit of friendship so deeply defined as here in the things of the spirit.

No man can save his brother's soul,
Nor pay his brother's debt.

Human friendship has limits because of the greatness of man. We are too big to be fully comprehended by another person. There is always something in us left unexplained and unexplored. Since we do not even know ourselves, much less can another person hope to probe into the recesses of our being. Friendship has a limit because of the infinite element in the soul. It is hard to kick against the pricks, but they are meant to drive us toward the true end of living. It is hard to be constrained by a limit in any area of life, but limits are designed to send us to a deeper and richer development of our life. Man's limitation is God's occasion. Only God can fully satisfy the hungry heart of man.

THE HIGHER FRIENDSHIP

CHAPTER NINE

The Higher Friendship

L ife is an education in love. There are grades and steps in it, occasions of varying opportunity for the discipline of love. It comes to us at many points, trying us at different levels, that it may get entrance somehow, and so make our lives not altogether a failure. When we give up our selfishness and isolation, even in the most rudimentary degree, we have made a beginning that is designed to carry us far, if we but follow the leading of our hearts.

There is an ideal toward which all our experience points. If it were not so, life would be a hopeless enigma and the world a meaningless farce. There must be a spiritual function intended, a design to build up strong and true moral character, to develop sweet and holy life, or else history is a despair and experience a hopeless riddle.

All truly great human life has been lived with a spiritual outlook and on a high level. Men have felt instinctively that there is no justification for all the pain and strife and failure and sorrow of the world if these do not serve a higher purpose than mere existence. Even our tenderest relationships need some more authoritative security than is to be found in themselves, even in the joy and hope they bring. That joy cannot be meant as an empty lure to keep life on the earth.

And spiritual man has also discovered that the very breakdown of human ties leads out to a larger and more permanent love. It is sooner or later found that the most perfect love cannot utterly satisfy the heart of man. All our human interrelationships, blessed and helpful as they may be, must necessarily be fragmentary and partial.

A man must discover that there is an infinite in him which only the infinite can match and supply. It is no disparagement of human friendship to admit this. It remains a blessed fact that it is possible to meet devotion, which makes us both humble and proud: humble at the sight of its noble sacrifice, proud with a glad pride at its wondrous beauty. Man is capable of the highest heights of love. But man can never take the place of God, and without God life is shorn of its glory and divested of its meaning.

So the human heart has ever craved for a relationship that is deeper and more lasting than any possible among men, undisturbed by change, unmenaced by death, unbroken by fear, unclouded by doubt. The limitations and losses of earthly friendship are meant to drive us to the higher friendship. Life is an education in love, but the education is not complete till we learn the love of the eternal. Ordinary friendship has done its work when the limits of friendship are reached, when through the discipline of love we are led into a larger love, when a door is opened out to a higher life.

The sickness of heart which is the lot of

all, the loneliness which not even the voice of a friend can dispel, the grief which seems to stop the pulse of life itself, find their final meaning in this compulsion toward the divine. We are sometimes driven out not knowing where we go, not knowing the purpose of it—only knowing through sheer necessity that here we have no abiding city or home or life or love, and seeking a city, a home, a life, a love that has foundations.

We have some training in the love of friends, as if only to prove to us that without love we cannot live. All our intimacies are but broken lights of the love of God. They are methods of preparation for the great communion. If our earthly friendships are helps to life, it is because they are saturated with the spiritual, and they prepare us by their very deficiencies for something more permanent. There have been implanted in man an instinct and a need which make him discontent until he finds contentment in God. If at any time we are forced to cease from man, whose breath is in his nostrils, it is that we may reach out to the infinite Father, unchanging, the same yesterday, today, and forever. This is the compelling need of man.

The solitude of life in its ultimate issue is because we were made for a higher companionship. It is in the innermost sanctuary, shut to every other visitant, that God meets us. We are driven to God by the needs of the heart. If the existence of God was due to a purely intellectual necessity, if we believed in Him only because our reason gave warrant for the faith, it would not matter much whether He really is and whether we really can know Him.

But when the instincts of our nature and the necessities of our heart-life demand God, we are forced to believe. In moments of deep feeling, when all pretense is silenced, a man may still be able to question the *existence* of God, but he does not question his own *need* of God. Man, to remain man, must believe in the possibility of this relationship with the divine. There is a love which passes the love of women, passes the love of comrades, passes all earthly love: the love of God to the weary, starved heart of man.

To believe in this great fact does not detract from human friendship, but really gives it worth and glory. It is because of this that all love has a place in the life of man. All our worships and friendships and loves come from God, and are but reflections of the divine tenderness. All that is beautiful and lovely and pure and of good repute finds its appropriate setting in God, for it was made by God. He made it for Himself. He made man with instincts, and aspirations, and heart-hunger, and divine unrest, that He might give them full satisfaction in Himself.

God claims everything, but He also gives everything. Our human relationships are sanctified and glorified by the spiritual union. He gives us back our kinships and friendships with a new light on them, an added tenderness, transfiguring our common ties and intimacies, flooding them with a heavenly joy. We part from men to meet with God so that we may be able to meet men again on a higher plane.

The love of God is the end and design of all other loves. If the flowers and leaves fade, it is that the time of ripe fruit is at hand. If these adornments are taken from the tree of life, it is to make room for the supreme fruit-age. Without the love of God all other love would be but deception, luring men on to awful disillusionment. We were born for the love of God; if we do not find it, it were better for us if we had never been born. We may have tasted all the joys the world can offer, have known success and the gains of success, been blessed with the sweetest friendships and the strongest loves, but if we have not found this the chief end of life, we have missed our chance, and can only have at the last a desolated life.

But if through the joy or through the sorrow of life, through love or the want of it, through the gaining of friends or the loss of them, we have been led to endow our lives with the friendship of God, we are possessed of the incorruptible and undefiled that passes not away. The man who has this has attained the secret cheaply even if it had to be purchased with his heart's blood, with the loss of his dream of blessedness. When the fabric of life crumbled to its native dust, and he rose out of its wreck, the vision of the eternal love came with the thrill of a great revelation. It was the entrance into the mystery; the wonder of it awed him and the joy of it inspired him, and he awakened to the fact that never again could he be *alone* to all eternity.

Communion with God is the great fact of life. All our forms of worship, all our ceremonies and symbols of religion, find their meaning here. It is true that there is an ethic of religion, certain moral teachings valuable for life; there are truths of religion to be laid hold of by reason; there are consolations of religion to comfort the heart; but the root of all religion is this mystical union, a communion with the Unseen, a friendship with God that is open to man.

Religion is not an acceptance of a creed or a burden of commandments but a personal secret of the soul, to be attained by each man for himself. It is the experience of the nearness of God, the mysterious contact with the divine, and the consciousness that we stand in a special individual relationship with Him. The first state of exaltation, when the knowledge burst upon the soul, of course cannot last, but its effect remains in inward peace and in outward motivation toward nobler life.

Men of all ages have known this close relationship. The possibility of it is the glory of life, and the fact of it is the romance and the true reading of history. All devout men who have ever lived have lived in the light of this communion. All religious experience has had in common the fact that somehow the soul is so possessed by God that doubt of His existence ceases. The task of life becomes to keep step with Him, so that there may be correspondence between the outer and the inner conditions of life. Men have known this communion in such a degree that they have been called the friends of God, but something of the experience which underlies the term is true of the pious of all generations.

To us, in our place in history, communion with God comes through Jesus Christ. It is an ineffable mystery, but it is still a fact of experience. Only through Jesus do we know God, His interest in us, His desire for us, His purpose with us. He not only shows us in His own example the blessedness of a life in fellowship with the Father, but He makes it possible for us. United to Jesus, we know ourselves united to God. The power of Jesus is not limited to the historical impression made by His life. It entered the world as history; it lives in the world as spiritual fact today. Luther's experience is the experience of all believers: "To me it is not simply an old story of an event that happened once; for it is a gift, a bestowing, that endures forever."

We offer Christ the submission of our hearts and the obedience of our lives, and He offers us His abiding presence. We take Him as our Master, and He takes us as His friends. "I call you no longer servants," He said to His disciples, "but I have called you friends." The servant knows not what his Master is doing, for his only duty is to obey; a friend is admitted to his Master's confidence, and though he may do the same thing as a servant, he does not do it any longer unreasoningly, but, having been taken into counsel, he knows why he is doing it. This was Christ's method with His disciples: not to apportion to each his task, but to show them His great purpose for the world, and to ask for their service and devotion to carry it out.

The distinction is not that a servant pleases his master and a friend pleases himself; it is that our Lord takes us up into a relationship of love with Himself, and we go out into life inspired with His spirit to work His work. It begins with the self-surrender of love; and love, not fear nor favor, becomes the motive. To feel thus the touch of God on our lives changes the world. Its fruits are joy, and peace, and confidence that all the events of life are suffused not only with meaning but with a meaning of love.

The higher friendship brings a satisfaction of the heart and a joy commensurate to the love. Its reward is itself—the sweet, enthralling relationship—and not any advantageous gain it promises, either in the present or for the future. Even if there were no physical or moral rewards and punishments in the world, we would still love and serve Christ *for His own sake*. The soul that is bound by this personal attachment to Jesus has a life in the eternal, which transfigures the life in time with a great joy.

We can see at once that to be the friend of God will also mean peace. It has brought peace over the troubled lives of all His friends throughout the ages. Every man who enters into His covenant knows the world to be a spiritual arena in which the love of God manifests itself. He walks no longer on a sodden earth and under a gray sky, for he knows that, though all men misunderstand him, he is understood and followed with loving sympathy in heaven.

It was this confidence in God as a real and near Friend which gave to Abraham's life such distinction and the calm repose which made his character so impressive. Strong in the sense of God's friendship, he lived above the world, prodigal of present possessions because sure of the future, waiting securely in the hope of the great salvation. He walked with God in sweet, unaffected piety and serene faith, letting his character ripen in the sunshine and living out his life as unto God and not unto men.

To know the love of God does not mean the impoverishing of our lives by robbing them

THE HIGHER FRIENDSHIP

It is worth all the care and
effort we can give to have and to
keep Him for our Friend who
will be a lasting possession,
whose life enters into the very
fiber of our life and whose love
makes us certain of God.

of their other sweet relations. Rather, it means the enriching of these by revealing their true beauty and purpose. Sometimes we are brought nearer God through our friends, if not through their influence or the joy of their love, then through the discipline which comes from their very limitations and from their loss. But oftener the experience has been that, through our union with the Friend of friends, we are led into richer and fuller communion with our fellows.

The nearer we get to the center of the circle, the nearer we get to each other. To be joined together in Christ is the only permanent union, deeper than the tie of blood, higher than the bond of kin, closer than the most sacred earthly relationship. Spiritual kinship is the great link to unite men. "Who are my brethren?" asked Jesus, and for answer pointed to His disciples, and added, "Whosoever shall do the will of my Father in heaven, the same is my mother and sister and brother."

We ought to make more of our Christian friendships, the communion of the saints, the fellowship of believers. "They that feared God spake often one with another," said the prophet Malachi in one of the darkest hours of religious history. What mutual comfort and renewed hope they would get from and give to each other! Faith can be increased and love stimulated and enthusiasm revived by true friendship.

The supreme friendship with Christ will not take from us any of our treasured intimacies (unless they are evil); it will increase the number of them and the true force of them. It will link us with all who love the same Lord in sincerity and truth. It will open our heart to the world of men that Jesus loved and gave His life to save.

This friendship with the Lord knows no fear of loss; neither life, nor death, nor things present, nor things to come can separate us. It is joy and strength in the present, and it lights up the future with a great hope. We are not much concerned about speculations regarding the future, for we know that we are in the hands of our Lover. All that we care to assert of the future is that Christ will in an ever fuller degree be the environment of all Christian souls, and the effect of that constant environment will fulfill the aspiration of the apostle, "We shall be like Him, for we shall see Him as He is."

Communion produces likeness. This even now is the test of our friendship with the Lord. Are we assimilating His mind, His way of looking at things, His judgments, His spirit? Is the Christ-conscience being developed in us? Have we an increasing interest in the things which interest Him, an increasing love of the things that He loves, an increasing desire to serve the purposes He has at heart? "Ye are my friends if ye do whatsoever I command you" is the test by which we can try ourselves.

Fellowship with Him, being much in His company, thinking of Him, seeking to please Him, will produce His likeness and will bring us together on more intimate terms. As love leads to the desire for fuller fellowship, so fellowship leads to a deeper love. Even if sometimes we almost doubt whether we are really in this blessed covenant of friendship, our policy is to go on loving Him, serving Him, striving to please Him, and we will yet receive the assurance which will bring peace; He will not disappoint us at the last. It is worth all the care and effort we can give to have and to keep Him for our Friend who will be a lasting possession, whose life enters into the very fiber of our life and whose love makes us certain of God.

We ought to use our faith in this friendship to bless our lives. To have an earthly friend whom we trust and reverence can be to us a source of strength, keeping us from evil and making us ashamed of evil. The dearer the friend and the more spiritual the friendship, the keener will be this feeling and the more needful to keep our garments clean.

It must reach its height of intensity and of moral effectiveness in the case of friendship with God. There can be no motive on earth so powerful. If we could only have such a friendship, we see at once what an influence it might have over our life. We can appreciate more than the joy and peace and comfort of it: We can feel the *power* of it. To know ourselves ever before a living, loving Presence, having a constant sense of Christ abiding in us, taking

Him with us into the marketplace, into our business and our pleasure, to have Him as our familiar Friend in joy and sorrow, in gain and loss, in success and failure, must, inevitably be a source of strength, lifting life to a higher level of thought and feeling and action.

Supposing it were true and possible, it would naturally be the strongest force in the world, the most effective motive that could be devised. It would affect the whole moral outlook, making some things easy that are now deemed impossible, and making some things impossible that now to our shame are too easy. Supposing this covenant with God were true, and we knew ourselves to have such a Lover of our soul, it would as a matter of course give us deeper and more serious views of human life, and yet at the same time take away from us the burden and unrest of life.

Unless history is a lie and experience a delusion, it *is* true. The world is vocal with a chorus of witnesses to the truth of God's covenant. From all kinds of men comes the testimony to its reality—from the old, who look forward to this Friend to make their bed in dying; from the young, who know His aid in the fiery furnace of temptation; from the strong, in the burden of the day and the dust of the battle, who know the rest of His love even in the sore labor; from the weak, who are mastered by His gracious pity and inspired by His power to suffer and to bear.

Christ's work on earth was to make the friendship of God possible to all. It seems too good to be true, too wondrous a condescension on His part, but its reality has been tested and attested by many generations of believers. This covenant of friendship is open to us, to be ours in life and in death and even past the gates of death.

The human means of communication is prayer, though we limit it sadly. Prayer is not merely an act of worship, the bending of the knee on set occasions and offering petitions in need. It is an attitude of soul, opening the life on the Godward side and keeping free communication with the world of spirit. It is possible to pray always, and to keep our friendship ever green and sweet, so that God comes back upon the life as dew upon the thirsty ground.

There is an interchange of feeling, a responsiveness of love, a thrill of mutual friendship.

You must love Him, ere to you
He shall seem worthy of your love.

The great appeal of the Christian faith is to Christian experience. Loving Christ is its own justification, as every loving heart knows. Life evidences itself: The existence of light is its own proof. The power of Christ on the heart needs no other argument than itself. Men only doubt when the life has died out, and the light has waned and flickered and spent itself. It is when there is no sign of the spirit in our midst, no token of forces beyond the normal and the usual, that we can deny the spiritual. It is when faith is not in evidence that we can dispute faith. It is when love is dead that we can question love.

The Christian faith is not a creed but a life, not a proposition but a passion. Love is its own witness to the soul that loves, even as communion is its own attestation to the spirit that lives in the fellowship. The man who lives with Jesus knows Him to be a Lover that cleaves closer than a brother, a Friend that loves at all times, and a Brother born for adversity.

It does not follow that there is an end of the questions, so far as we are concerned, if we say that we at least do not know that friendship, and cannot love Him. Some even say it with a wistful longing: "Oh, that I knew where I might find Him." It is true that love cannot be forced, that it cannot be made to order, that we cannot love because we ought or even because we want. But we can bring ourselves into the presence of the lovable. We can enter into friendship through the door of discipleship; we can learn love through service; and the day will come to us also when the Master's word will be true, "I call you no longer servant, but I call you friend."

His love will take possession of us till all else seems as hatred in comparison. "All lovers blush when ye stand beside Christ," says Samuel Rutherford; "woe unto all love but the love of Christ. Shame forevermore be upon all glory but the glory of Christ; hunger forevermore be upon all heaven but Christ. I cry death,

death be upon all manner of life but the life of Christ."

To be called *friends* by our Master, to know Him as the Lover of our souls, to give Him entrance to our hearts, is to learn the meaning of living and to experience the ecstasy of living. The Higher Friendship is bestowed without money and without price, and is open to every heart responsive to God's great love.